D1207940

BOB FELLER
Hall of Fame Strikeout Star

BOB FELLER

Hall of Fame Strikeout Star

By GENE SCHOOR

DOUBLEDAY & COMPANY, INC.
GARDEN CITY, NEW YORK

336755

MITCHELL MEMORIAL LIBRARY
MISSISSIPPI STATE UNIVERSITY

Library of Congress Catalog Card Number 62–11452
Copyright © 1962 by Gene Schoor
All Rights Reserved
Printed in the United States of America

336755

MITCHELL MEMORIAL LIBRARY
MISSISSIPPI STATE UNIVERSITY

BOB FELLER
Hall of Fame Strikeout Star

CHAPTER ONE

From the first day the infant Bob Feller could crawl in his crib, there was a ball for him to play with—to push, to prod, to pick up, to toss.

Even his mother, exasperated by the rabid baseball fervor in her own household before marriage, couldn't conceal her pride in the firm way Bob's fingers curled around the toy ball playfully extended to him. A strong baby, she exulted.

It was only the natural grasping instinct of an infant, but who could tell that to the beaming father and the admiring relatives. Her dad had been a prominent ballplayer in Iowa and even now, near seventy, could step out and still throw the fast one.

Brother Ed still played professional baseball and had been considered good enough for a major league trial. As for Bill, he had never forgotten his diamond dreams.

"Look at the size of those hands," chortled Grandpop Foret.

"He's gonna be a catcher," said Uncle Ed, "or maybe a first baseman."

The baby, gurgling in glee at the adult attention, flipped the toy ball out of the crib.

"A pitcher!" his father laughed. "And he's wild already."

But all through the years of Bob's infancy and early child-hood, Bill Feller carefully concealed the smouldering ambition he had for his son.

"I won't make him a baseball player," he told his wife after a grueling day on the farm when everything had gone wrong. "I won't force it down his gullet. But, by God, if he has it in him and he wants it, I'll help him like no father ever did before."

By the time Bob was five, it was so obvious which way the twig was bent that Bill Feller no longer needed to bother masking his hopes.

A sturdy farm boy with a solemn face and lively eyes, Bob's greatest fun was playing ball. He could stand for hours tossing a ball against the barn or toss stones for distance out in the fields.

At first, Bill stayed clear, merely observing and insuring a plentiful supply of rubber balls, but after a while he'd hurry in from the chores to play a bit of catch with Bob before the evening sun went down.

On trips to town with his mom or dad, young Bob always wangled one or the other into buying him a new ball. He enjoyed hearing Grandpa Foret's baseball tales of the days when he was "the best durned pitcher in Ioway."

It wasn't all "Play Ball" on the Feller farm. Corn doesn't grow by itself and cows don't walk up to the bottles and squirt milk. Horses have to be fed, fields plowed, crops harvested, chickens tended, machinery repaired. Bill worked slave hours on his 360 acres.

But conscientiously as he tended his farm duties, Bill Feller managed to find time for baseball with his son. This devotion to a game, even in baseball-mad Van Meter, became first a local joke and then a legend.

Farmer friends would walk up to Bill and slyly ask how the baseball crop was doing. He took his ribbing amiably and with such conviction of ultimate reward that the gloss soon rubbed off the joke and everyone accepted the fact that young Feller would be a baseball star.

Bob did his share of the work. A boy grows up clean and strong on a farm and Bob laid the foundation for his tremendous arm and back muscle development there. He fished and he hunted, and he loafed, too, like all little boys.

He went to school in Van Meter and it wasn't long before his classmates knew that Bob Feller didn't hanker to be a fireman, engineer, soldier, or explorer as they did. His ambition was the major leagues, as a player traveling from city to city, being paid for having fun.

These were the things he absorbed from his dad as they grew closer to each other, playing ball and talking it over, not as fellow dreamers but as long-range planners.

Bill Feller rushed in from the fields at lunch time, bolting his food in order to get in a few throws with Bob. Supper warmed on the stove every evening as they worked out behind the barn and Mom endured it with the patience of a woman who had always lived through this.

This philosophy became an integral part of this dedicated lad. One day at the age of eight in the third grade, asked to write a composition, Bob responded with this extraordinary glimpse into the hidden recesses of a boy's desire:

MY LIFE

When I was a tree, with my brothers and sisters there were many of us, but there is not many of us now. Many

9

of us have been cut down and made into lumber and it came my turn and they cut me down and made me into a big board and Mr. Stuck's manual training boys got me and made me into a home plate on the baseball diamond, and that's the end.

For all her faith and love in her husband, Margaret Feller had a deeply practical strain and did not regard the growing emphasis on baseball without qualms.

She voiced her doubts one night, after another late, warmed-over meal delayed by a father-son catch behind the barn.

"Bill," she began hesitantly, "about Bob . . ."

Bill peered up from a farm catalogue. There was a new machine, a combine, he was thinking about that could save a lot of time on the farm if he planted wheat instead of corn. . . .

"I'm worried, Bill," she said, dropping her sewing. "You know . . . all this baseball . . . and Bob so young . . . and I . . ."

"Mom," Bill answered gently, "stop worrying. You can't grow wheat out of corn seed. I'm a farmer and I plant and I till and I help it along, but I can't grow something that isn't there. It's the same with Bob. He'll be what he has to be."

He spoke with unexpected intensity.

"He's only a kid, but I tell you he's got something special. I know baseball and I know Bob. He can be somebody if we give him some help."

Bill leaned forward, speaking earnestly, a light kindling in his sharp eyes. "I've watched him and studied him, the way he moves, the way he throws, his rhythm, his co-ordination . . ."

It was the sort of talk she remembered her own mother putting up with for years in a home where baseball was the gospel. "Bill," she broke in, "where can it get him?"

"Off the farm and into a decent life," he answered quickly.

"Here, he has something solid and real," she continued. "If he doesn't want to be a farmer, he can get an education and go into something else. I just don't want him disappointed and hurt later on, led on by a dream . . ."

"Like me, you mean?" he asked bitterly.

"Now Bill, it's you I'm thinking about too. Putting your whole life into making Bob a ballplayer. What if he doesn't make it. How about you? And Bob?"

"That's just it, Mom. It's better than what happened to me. I never got my chance. Maybe I would have made it and maybe not. But I never found out and it'll always eat me."

How true for poor Bill, she thought.

"I know Bob can get to the top some day," he went on, "but if he doesn't, it won't be because either of us failed him. That's important too."

So the worried mother of an eight-year-old baseball player nodded assent, but with a heart filled with concern at what to her seemed at best a gamble with a son's future.

She resumed her sewing, and Bill turned back to the catalogue and his labor-saving plans to gain more time for the daily game of catch with Bob.

CHAPTER TWO

It was a typical early summer evening at the Feller farm.

Mom was puttering around the kitchen, wondering how long she would have to keep the supper warming on the stove. Bobby, aged nine, his chores completed, sat dreamy-eyed on the porch, a ball and mitt by his side, waiting for Dad to come home.

Bill Feller, clucking the horses in after a hard day in the burning sun, moved with a strange mixture of impatience and exhilaration. He hadn't realized how much he looked forward to these twilight catches with Bob.

Bob's long face with his full mouth and dimpled chin broke into smiling radiance when his father came into view from behind the barn.

"Dad," he shouted, "boy, I've been waiting! Let's get going!"

Bill Feller grinned in secret delight. The kid loves it as much as I do, he thought.

"Hold up, sonny," he yelled back. But he waited as Bob ran to him with the gloves and ball. "Let's get these horses in and we'll be ready."

12

The sun was an orange-red ball scorching the western horizon, but the light was strong as Bobby and his dad began warming up. Bill's workaday weariness vanished as he half-squatted behind the plate.

The young squirt, he thought. He's really throwing hard. The kid, gazing at him with the exaggerated earnestness of youth, wound up to throw. He narrowed his eyes like a big league pitcher, pumped his arms forward, then back and over his head, his right arm reaching back as his left leg rose. Then, zing—Bob came down hard and let the ball go.

Smack!

The ball slammed into the pocket with a thud. No doubt about it—the ball hurt.

"Nice throwing, Bobby," the father conceded. The little devil certainly had a strong arm. The motion wasn't too good, Bill thought, not enough back and shoulder in it, but the pitch came in with a wallop.

"That's my Lefty Grove pitch," Bobby shouted exuberantly.

"You're no Lefty," Bill jibed the youngster.

"Nope, I'm Righty Feller. Ol' Righty Feller on the mound."

Bill laughed. "Let's try some infield practice." He began throwing easy grounders to the boy.

Bob, his eyes fixed on the ball, crouched into position, glove waiting scooplike for the bounding sphere. He was up an instant after the catch, firing the ball to his father as though the fastest man in the big leagues was racing down the line to first base.

"Got 'im," he'd yell if the ball went true. More often than not Bob's hurried throws went wide or high, whanging against the side of the barn.

It was almost dark when they stopped, and Bill could sense his wife hovering impatiently at the kitchen door. "Guess that's enough," he told Bob. "Let's git 'fore Mom beats our brains out with the bat."

They walked toward the frame house, an odd pair, this small rabbity lad with overalls and baseball cap, a tired farmer trudging along in his work clothes.

Something was bothering Bill.

"Wonder how far you can throw the ball, son," he said. They were almost at the porch when Bill stopped suddenly.

"Let's just try one, for the fun of it," he grunted, almost to himself. "Over in the pasture there."

Puzzled, Bob looked up, but followed obediently.

Bill Feller scraped a line on the bare ground with his heavy work shoes, then turned to his son.

"I want you to throw as far out there as you can," he said. "Put everything you've got into it. Then we'll measure the distance."

Bob's eyes lit up. "Hey, that's a great idea. Okay, watch me go."

His boyish features set grimly as he tensed for the effort. Bob gripped the ball tightly, hunched forward, rocked backward in a throwing rhythm, dropped his right arm behind him, then whirled forward and threw with all his strength.

The ball shot out in a high arc, a whirling grayish blob plummeting through the soft night air, hardly visible as it reached its apex and began to drop, then finally landed somewhere far out on the cropped ground behind the haystack.

Some throw, Bill thought in amazement. He stared, thunderstruck.

"How're you gonna measure it, Dad?" Bob asked.

"Get me that fifty foot of new line I bought the other day," Bill finally answered. "It's in the shed. And better bring a lantern."

Bob rushed back with the rope and lantern and they began searching for the ball. Bill found the worn old rocket on a clump of grass. Silently they stretched the line and worked their way back to the take-off spot. Bill stood silent for a few moments when they completed the measuring.

He wouldn't believe it—275 feet!

Bill felt his son tugging at his sleeve. Dimly, he heard the boy's voice, a note of alarm in it.

"Pop, what's the matter—Pop!"

"Nothing, son," he said slowly. He put his hand on Bob's head, affectionately pulled the peak of his cap over the boy's eyes.

They started back to the house, hastened by the rapping on the tin door that signaled the end of Mom's patience.

"How much was it, Dad?" Bob asked.

"A lot, Bobby—275 feet."

"Is that good?" The boy wanted to please his father more than anyone else in the world.

Bill patted the youngster's shoulder.

"Better'n any other nine-year-old kid in Iowa, I'll bet," he said.

Father and son never were closer than at that moment, walking through the dusk to the cheery brightness gleaming through the open kitchen door and to the long delayed meal.

CHAPTER THREE

The next day Bill Feller drove into town as soon as he could get away from the farm and was gone for two hours.

His wife repressed a smile at Bill's furtive return laden with packages and his hasty explanation. "Got some things for Bob," he said, moving quickly past her to the boy's room.

She said nothing to Bob when he came home from school, late as usual now that he stayed to play ball with the other boys before hitching a ride or walking back.

"Where's Dad?" Bob asked, gulping his milk and home-baked bread and jam.

"Down at the Raccoon," she answered. "Drawing water."

"Guess I better go and help," he said.

"Change your clothes, then," she said, bending down to kiss the back of his neck. "You know how muddy it always is down there."

The Raccoon meandered through the Feller property, a narrow stream which supplied water for the livestock. The ground was too mushy to bring the truck closer than 200 yards and the water had to be hauled laboriously by pail to the big tank in the truck.

Each bucket held several gallons and water can get awfully heavy after a number of trips, but Bob kept pace with his dad, one pail to the older man's two. Only a few years later, Bob was carting two just like his dad.

"That's enough," Bill finally said. Bob emptied the bucket into the tank with a sigh of relief, turning to his father and waiting for the words which had become a ritual with them.

"Feel up to a catch?" Bill would say with a straight face betrayed only by the twinkle in his eyes.

And Bob would scurry to wherever he had hidden the ball and gloves, toss the mitt to his father, don his own glove, then release all his pent-up exuberance into an enormous umpirical shout of "Play Ba-a-a-ll!"

Bill grinned, got the truck rolling, and drove back. Instead of proceeding directly to the barn and unloading the water, he pulled up in front of the house. Bob gazed at him, puzzled.

"Hop out and see if there's anything under your bed," his father said. Bob looked blank for a moment, then comprehension dawned. "Wow!"

He leaped from the truck and raced in. All boys love surprises and Bob sensed this one was something particularly pleasant and special.

Bill waited for his son to discover the boxes and their contents, enjoying the anticipation almost as much as the explosion of joyous sounds which came from the house.

"Mom, Mom, Dad," Bob shouted, running from his room. "Look what I got. Look . . . Look . . ."

Bill saw the boy appear in the doorway, the new baseball cap on his head, the uniform in his hands. Bob stopped on the porch, dropped the spiked shoes and modeled the uniform against his body, as if he already were wearing it.

"Boy," he exclaimed, "look at that."

Bob gazed down at himself, then at his father.

"Thanks, Dad," he said, suddenly calm. "Thanks a million."

Bill could only manage a smile and nod, surprised at the choking emotion suddenly welling in him.

"Put it on, Son," he said at last. "I'll be waiting behind the barn." He drove off and Bob scampered inside to change.

Donning the suit, Bob posed before the mirror. He wound up and pitched. He swung the bat. He scooped up hot grounders. And he made the myriad grimaces of a big leaguer in action—the narrowed eyes of a hurler looking for the sign, the grimness of the clean-up hitter at bat in the crucial moment.

Finally, he strutted out into the kitchen, boyishly proud but a mite embarrassed, too, in front of his mother.

She turned from the stove to admire her boy.

"It's beautiful," she said.

"Not beautiful, Mom," he corrected, but glowing just the same. "Baseball uniforms aren't beautiful!"

"But you are," she laughed, hugging him.

The suit was as close to regulation as Bill could buy for a nine-year-old boy. It was gray flannel with a thin vertical stripe and red piping along the shirt front. He wore striped red stockings and a cap with a scarlet peak.

"Spikes, too, Mom," Bob added, dangling the black leather baseball shoes before her. "And a Rogers Hornsby glove for me and a Ray Schalk catcher's mitt for Dad."

He showed them with the reverence of a young boy for a genuine leather glove, tanned and gleaming in its newness. One glove looked like any other to Mrs. Feller, but as a

18

mother she gloated and enthused with him over these incalculable treasures.

"Real major league baseballs," he continued, revealing two shiny, white horsehide spheres. "And a Louisville slugger bat."

"I suppose I can expect the both of you later than ever for supper," his mother sighed, returning to reality. "Now, I'm warning—"

"Aw, Mom," Bob cut in. "You can eat supper any time, but you gotta have light to play ball."

Put that way, the logic was unassailable. "Don't worry, Mom," he went on, pecking her cheek to clinch the argument. "We'll be in as soon as it's dark."

"It's a good thing the sun sets every night," she countered affectionately, but he was gone and she felt the same sense of baffled wonderment at this single-minded devotion to baseball as all the Feller friends and neighbors.

Bob felt like a big leaguer throwing to his father, that evening. The feel of the uniform clinging to his small body, the glove on his hand, the compact tightness of the expensive baseball, all gave him a radiant joy that shone in his young face.

"Wear it to school tomorrow," his father said. "Change into your spikes when you get out. But don't trip over 'em."

Bob's outfit was the sensation of the fourth grade the next day. His classmates gathered around him and even Bob's teacher, Miss Wycoff, a kindly soul who knew a lot more about boys than she did about baseball, complimented his appearance.

"You really want to be a baseball player, don't you, Bob?" she asked.

"Yes, ma'am," he answered.

"It's a nice game," she smiled. "You can't grow baseballs and you can't eat them, but if it makes you happy and doesn't interfere with the serious things, I suppose it's all right."

His new equipment plus his natural athletic superiority now established Bob as the kingpin of his group on the diamond. He owned the bat and balls and was manager and captain, with a choice of position.

He preferred third base or shortstop because even at nine, he liked the long throw across the diamond. Rogers Hornsby and Babe Ruth were the slugging idols of the day and, considering himself quite a hitter too, Bob always batted cleanup.

Although he also admired Lefty Grove's accomplishments immensely, Bob had no serious thoughts or ambitions about pitching. The fact is that he had never discussed or thought of any particular position. He just wanted to play baseball.

His father spent as much time with him on fielding and batting as he did with throwing. Bill gave up his own horseshoe pitching, at which he was a community crackerjack, to devote time to his son's baseball training.

He even rigged up two powerful arc lamps behind the barn so they could play a bit longer after the sun had set. It meant a longer workout and a longer delay with supper for Mrs. Feller.

But her complaints, reduced to a resigned murmur, went ignored in the amiable but insistent way of men who know their duty and would not be swayed from it.

CHAPTER FOUR

The summers slipped by quickly and pleasantly. The Fellers worked their farm, played baseball at dusk and week ends, talked baseball through the cold winter months.

Bob, taller and heavier, now was eleven years old. A sister, Marguerite, had joined the family a year before, a joyous arrival who in no way interfered with the daily baseball routine.

Bill Feller had devised a way to foil the elements when they turned unfavorable. He cleared enough space inside the barn for them to practice in defiance of the weather.

Somewhere and somehow their evening catch passed from random play to purposeful endeavor. Bill fashioned a home plate and built a toe slab at the regulation pitching distance. He taught Bob everything he knew about the technique of the game—hitting, bunting, fielding, running the bases, strategy.

If Bill Feller harbored notions of developing his son into a pitcher, he kept it secret from Bob as well as himself. He hewed only to making Bob a well-rounded ballplayer. He tore apart a chicken coop to salvage the wire mesh and wood for a batting cage. He threw grounders to the boy, had him scoop up the ball and throw to first base in one easy motion.

The Feller neighbors frankly thought Bill had gone mad. The sight of the two, adult and boy, armed with lanterns searching the pasture in the dark for baseballs would convince any doubter.

With a stock of only a half dozen baseballs, this was a necessity. Batting practice was a constant march from plate to pasture and back again. Bob would hit five or six balls, then both would retrieve. No matter how ludicrous it seemed to others, it made sense to them.

Naturally all this practice session delayed supper later than ever, but Mrs. Feller, occupied with her baby daughter, had no time or inclination to fret. She had given up on the males of the Feller household.

Bob was in sixth grade and a familiar figure at the school playground when the Van Meter High School baseball coach approached him late one afternoon.

A stocky, gray-haired man with lively eyes that missed nothing, he had studied the eager youngster. He noted Bob's movements in the field and his fierce swings at bat. Moreover, the kid threw pretty hard, he thought.

"Are you the Feller boy?" he asked with a friendly smile.

"Yes, sir," Bob answered, jiggling the ball in his hand.

"Know who I am?" the man continued.

"Yes, sir," Bob said, puzzled but interested. The high school coach might just as well be Miller Huggins or John McGraw, Bob thought, even if he did know him.

"You know all the good grade school players, don't you," the man went on. "Can you get up a team?"

Bob's heart leaped wildly. Could he! Speechless, he managed to nod assent.

"Good," the coach said to the startled lad. "Get your club together and be at our field tomorrow after school."

"Who—who are we playing?" Bob stammered.

"The Van Meter varsity, that's who." The coach grinned widely and departed, leaving Bob goggle-eyed.

Van Meter High, drawing from a rural community which could not always spare its sons from farm chores, usually was at a disadvantage against league rivals from larger towns. The local coach realized his team needed game experience and that even grade school youngsters would be better than no opposition at all.

As the hardest thrower on his team, Bob became the pitcher. No doubt of it, he could fire the ball. His catcher's hand was raw and puffed in a few innings. The batters had it even rougher. Bob just blazed the ball past them.

Several times his dad sneaked off the farm to watch Bob pitch against the high school team, occasionally jotting notes. When the boy returned home, Bill discussed whatever flaws he had spotted.

The coach knew Bill and, noticing him in the stands one day, ambled over.

"Nice kid you've got there," he opened.

Bill smiled his thanks, but said nothing.

"I hear you've been teaching him," the coach said.

"Just having a little fun," Bill shrugged it off. "We both like to play ball."

"The kid's got a wonderful arm," the coach continued. "He throws real hard. Knows what to do. I like the way he handles himself out there. He's a real ballplayer."

He paused while they watched Bob loosen up on the sidelines.

"I'll tell you something, Mr. Feller," he said after a while. "I could use that boy on my club right now. He's better than half my team."

Bill only smiled. It won't be long, he thought, before all of them will be saying that.

"If you'd like," the coach said, "I know the manager of the American Legion team over at Adel. How about Bob playing for them this summer? He needs some team play, and he could learn an awful lot."

Bill promised to talk it over with Bob, and the coach turned back to his team. Bill only advised, but Bob would have to make the decisions. It was always that way between them.

Bob's team played eight practice games against the Van Meter varsity that spring and won seven. But young Feller still hadn't decided on becoming a pitcher. He played third base a lot and center field, where his strong arm showed to good advantage.

The last day of school was an exciting event in Van Meter. High school and grade school students combined on a picnic. It was fun. Box lunches. Races. Sings. Horseshoe pitching. Baseball.

Bob brought his bat and ball and before long one of the teachers, a husky fellow who could pole a long ball, was belting out flies. Bob was shagging in the field and throwing the ball back.

A crowd soon gathered to watch the young sixth-grader fire the ball on a line no matter how far it was hit. Gradually the other fielders dropped out and it became a contest between man and boy.

The teacher, his muscles bulging and sweat pouring down

24

him, was putting everything into his wallops and getting a lot of distance. But Bob would move easily into position, camp under the fly, catch it firmly, take one step forward, and zing! The ball would be cutting the air like an arrow.

"This kid is phenomenal," the young teacher said finally, dropping his bat. "I've never seen any boy throw like that. Why he's got an arm that's as good as any pro player I've ever seen."

The crowd laughed, but everyone applauded when Bob trotted in to pick up his bat and rejoin the group. Bob fled embarrassed, but his father, watching from a comfortable spot in the shade of a tree off to the side, felt like shouting out to everyone the love and pride for his boy.

With the school term over, Bob joined the Legion team at Adel, a nearby town much larger than Van Meter. He played shortstop and center field mostly, handling himself with a maturity beyond his meager eleven years. It was only a matter of days before the town buzzed over his sensational plays.

Stationed in center in a Legion game one day, Feller came up with an outstanding catch and even more sensational throw to catch the runner at the plate.

It was the ninth inning of a tight game, Adel leading by two runs, but a man on third and the rivals' slugger at bat. The local Babe Ruth connected and the ball headed deep and far to Bob's left.

Bob was off with the crack of the bat. It looked like a sure hit, possibly a homer. Bob dug in and raced after it. At the last moment on the dead run, he stabbed with his glove and caught the ball.

The man on third tagged up and sped for home. Bob

whirled and threw in one motion, putting everything into the peg. It seemed hopeless, even to Bob, as he watched the ball bullet toward the plate.

The ball sped fast and low. The runner hit the dirt in a big slide, but the catcher was waiting with the ball.

"Yer out," the umpire bawled, making the familiar thumbs-up motion.

The spectators roared in amazement at the magnificent strike Feller had flung from deep center. Few runners took a chance advancing on Bob's arm, after that. When he played third, the first baseman usually complained that Feller was throwing too hard.

Bill Feller was very happy over Bob's continued improvement. The barber shop crowd no longer twitted him. His boy had earned a respect that made Bill's heart ache with joy.

Had the time come, Bill wondered, for a decision. Bob was young, of course, but perhaps it might be better to work toward a definite goal. He would have to talk to the boy.

That night, sitting on the porch in the soft summer air, Bill spoke up.

"How do you like pitching?" he asked.

"Pretty good," Bob answered. "While you're in there."

"It's fun, isn't it?"

"Sure," Bob grinned. "Especially when you strike someone out."

"As much fun as hitting a homer, would you say?" Bill persisted.

Bob pondered for a moment, then laughed. "Gee, Dad, I don't hit enough of 'em to know. But I sure like to hit. I like to get up there at the plate and smack that ball. It's a great feeling."

They sat for a while. Then Bill spoke softly.

"I think you're a good hitter and a good fielder," he said. "Don't get me wrong. But you throw better than you do anything else. Maybe that's what you ought to do. Son, you have all the making of a fine pitcher. You're strong and your fast ball is alive. Pitching is great fun."

Bob was quiet, gazing into the blackness spangled by pinpoint flickerings of stars millions of miles away. He heard the cattle stirring in the shed, the night creatures rustling in the fields, and the crickets. The future was a million miles away, too.

"I like pitching fine, Dad," he said at last. "Only, I wouldn't be in the game as much. You know, pitchers don't play every day. I love to play."

It was something Bill could understand.

"I know," he said, "but it's time you started to plan ahead. A pitcher is the most important man on the team. Not everyone can be a pitcher."

"You know best, Dad," Bob agreed.

Young Feller never doubted that Father knew best, then or later.

CHAPTER FIVE

Bill Feller blinked as he came out of the doctor's office into the strong sunlight of Van Meter.

His side still ached in its stiff strapping of tape and his eyes were slightly blurred by the drops. But nothing could dampen the feeling of elation coursing through him.

The gaunt, solemn face masked a spirit bursting with cheer as Bill strode through the bustling main street in a lumbering gait that bespoke years behind the plow.

"I must be soft in the head," he thought wryly, "to laugh at two broken ribs!"

Surely, Doc thought him crazy. Doc's expression had been as transparent as glass.

"How'd you get this?" he had asked while his strong fingers probed the huge throbbing bruise above Bill's hip.

Feller winced as he answered. "Missed one of Bob's fast ones," he said. "Hey, that hurts."

"It should," Doc snorted. "You've got two fractured ribs. Dawggont it, Bill, don't you know better than to play ball at your age?"

"Just having a catch, Doc," Bill explained lamely as the

physician deftly taped the injured area. But the remark had struck a chord.

Could age have something to do with it, Bill wondered. Missing the pitch worried Bill. The light was good and the ball came in terribly fast, or so it seemed. It glanced off the mitt and struck him on the left side.

But if his eyes were off a bit . . . maybe that was it!

"That's it," he exclaimed, startling the doctor. "Maybe I ought to have my eyes examined."

"More likely it's your head that needs examining," Doc retorted. But he put in the eye drops and tested Bill's vision.

"Perfect," he announced, finally. "Which is more than I can say for your sense."

Bill grinned. Perfect eyesight. It meant Bob really was throwing faster. Too fast for Bill to handle. And the kid only thirteen.

"Stop grinning," Doc commanded, reading his patient's thoughts. Everyone in town knew what went on in the Feller skull. That fool game of baseball and turning his son Bob into a professional ballplayer.

"Bob's thirteen now, isn't he?" Doc asked as he helped Bill into his clothes. "Beginning to sprout, I guess."

Bill finished dressing. Doc leaned back in his desk chair and regarded him thoughtfully.

"I hear you're planting wheat these days," he said. "More money in corn, isn't there?"

"Sure is, Doc," Bill answered, his thin features curling in a tight smile, "but wheat's a heap faster work."

Then, understanding Doc's real question, he added, "Gives me more time with my boy. More pleasure raising Bob than

29

raising corn. Money ain't everything and, besides, no one's starving at my place."

Perhaps this simple farmer does have the right philosophy of living, Doc thought sadly. Boyhood years are fleeting and Bill Feller wasn't wasting them. Doc, whose children had grown up without seeing too much of him, suddenly envied Bill Feller.

He slapped Bill Feller on the back and sent him out.

Bill drove home by reflex more than awareness. An idea which had taken root last winter was beginning to grow into interesting flower. He thought about it all the way back to the farm.

It had been hot stove league talk when the world lay frozen and forbidding outside, too cold for anything but idle talk in the warm kitchen. They had decided Bob would concentrate on becoming a pitcher, which wasn't really news to either.

Bill was sipping coffee and Bob languidly munching an apple when Mrs. Feller bustled in. "What are you two big executives settling now?" she quipped in deference to their solemn attitude at the table.

"Talking business, Mom," Bob answered.

"What kind of business?" she asked, not truly curious. She knew what their subject inevitably was.

"Men's business," Bob said. At thirteen, Bob already could sense the subtle encroachment on masculine supremacy.

"Hmmmph!" She smiled as she clattered among the pots and pans. "If you two attended more to business on the farm . . ."

No one took offense. Mon was so good-natured about her digs, and it was too cozy and warm indoors to fret.

"You know," Bill said, after a while, looking at his wife, "baseball is a big business too. Maybe . . ."

"Now, Bill," she said, turning in alarm, "don't you go getting strange ideas."

"Tain't so strange," Bill remarked. "But don't worry—yet."

What he hadn't said aloud was the notion to build his own ball park right there on the farm. Get up his own team, with Bob starring on it, and playing clubs from other towns.

But it was only a winter thought and Bill had forgotten about it until today's visit to the doctor. Bob was ready for more than catches behind the barn and high school competition in Van Meter.

That night Bill made up his mind and he broke the exciting news to his son.

"You throw hard enough to knock down a bull," he told Bob. "We've got to get you a team and I know just how to do it."

The plan was to build a baseball field on the flat ground behind the grove of oak trees overlooking the Raccoon River. As his practical mind grappled with the idea, Bill's enthusiasm mounted.

"We'll clear the pasture," he said, picturing the field in his mind. "We'll disc and roll it nice and flat, put up some stands, and sell hot dogs and soda."

Even at thirteen, Bob could forget dignity to jump in glee.

"What'll we call it, Dad?" he asked. "How about Feller Stadium? Wouldn't that be something!"

Bill laughed with him. "And wouldn't the neighbors be petitioning to have me put away for that one!" he shouted. "Nope, we'll call it something like Oak Park or maybe Raccoon Field."

31

"I got it," Bob cried. "How about Oak View Park?"

And so the field was christened and the venture born.

The Fellers were hard at work after the thaw. In addition to the spring planting, they built a baseball field. They leveled and scraped the ground. They cut saplings for fence posts and bought chicken wire by the rolls to fence it in. They built a scoreboard and sent to Des Moines for regulation bags for the bases.

The neighbors now were certain Bill Feller had lost his mind. They kidded him, but privately expressed pity for the poor neglected wife and family. Riding past the farm to view Feller's folly became a favorite Sunday diversion.

Bill never was happier than when working on the field. He built sturdy backstop and wire fences which ran 150 feet or so down the baselines. The infield had no grass, but it was leveled and raked a thousand times to sift out the stones.

Bill had rounded up a team and the day before the gala opening came home with twelve uniforms. Bob, by far the youngest of the aggregation, strutted like a peacock. He couldn't take his eyes off the bold lettering which spelled Oak Views across the chest.

Wisely, Bill did not use Bob on the mound. The youngster played shortstop, and quite creditably. The Oak Views got off to a fast start, winning their first six games with Bob hitting and fielding well.

The Sunday games drew good attendance, surprisingly. Now the neighbors who had scoffed, quickly changed course and began figuring Bill Feller's fortune; seeing crowds, sometimes as many as 1,000 at a game, paying thirty-five cents admission and buying refreshments, the hooters were transformed into rooters.

The sad truth is that Feller didn't make money. There were many expenses the envious neighbors didn't know about, but Bill wasn't concerned with more than breaking even. All he wanted was the opportunity to help Bob develop.

Bob played shortstop all that year and again in 1933, batting .321 with a number of extra-base wallops that season. He didn't set any records with his play at short, but he was reliable and he did throw bullets across the diamond.

Bill Feller didn't think his son was ready for the mound yet and, for that matter, Bob didn't want to pitch. He felt more comfortable in the infield and, besides, he could play every day.

But there was, as always, a shortage of good hurlers and Bill had to hire pitchers. The other performers were happy to play for the fun of it, but pitchers demanded money.

It was early in the spring of 1934 when Bob, aged fifteen, went to the mound for the first time in a regulation game.

CHAPTER SIX

The Oak Views were playing the local team at Winterset, Iowa, not far from Van Meter. It was a Sunday game and attracted a large crowd, mostly folks curious to see Bill Feller, the farmer who had built a baseball field for his son.

It was a chilly spring day despite a bright sun. At shortstop, Bob briskly slapped his fist into his glove to keep warm as he watched the Oak Views' new left-hander pitch. It was a tryout and not going too well.

The left-hander had nothing on the ball and served up too many good pitches. Lucky breaks and snappy fielding kept him out of serious trouble during the first two innings, but the Winterset team clouted the ball hard in the third.

Two hits and a walk filled the bases and Bill Feller got off the bench and walked toward the mound. Idly, Bob wondered what was going to happen.

The young shortstop scooped up a few pebbles and juggled them as he watched his father talk to the pitcher, then look back at the bench. Suddenly he realized his father was beckoning to him.

Bob trotted over to the mound as the lefty slouched off the diamond.

"We're stuck, Bob," his father said in a low voice. "How about it, I'm going to have you pitch. I think it's about time, don't you?"

Bob shrugged. "Okay," he said, hoping he appeared calmer than he felt.

"Just pour it in," Bill said tersely, the anxiety apparent in his tense face. "All you have to do is get the ball over the plate. Your fast ball is too much for these guys. Just take it nice and easy. Don't work too hard. Remember it's the first time you're pitching in a real game."

His dad looked so worried it suddenly struck Bob funny and he laughed. Somehow the tension dropped.

"Don't fret, Dad," he said. "This is just another catch behind the barn."

Bob turned to the plate and began his warmup. The ball hummed into the catcher's mitt with a loud smack. Bob was nervous, but not scared. Determination was written on the full, round, boyish face.

"Ready, Bob?" the umpire asked. Bob nodded.

The batter, a husky farm lad, stepped to the plate, swinging his bat ferociously.

Bob tugged the peak of his cap, watched for the sign from the catcher. His arms went overhead in the windup. He reared back and then let the pitch go. The bat swished through the air too late. Strike one.

Bob stole a glance at the bench. His dad sat hunched and taut, eyes riveted on the mound. Bob put too much on the next pitch and it was high for a ball. He wound up slowly and sent the next one sizzling in just over the knees for strike two.

"Get him, boy, get him!" Bob heard his teammates talking

it up behind him and vague noises from the stands. His arms pumped again, he bore down hard and the ball plummeted in and over before the hitter could move his bat.

"Strike three—yer out!"

The sweetest words in the world. Bob couldn't help turning to his father and grinning. Bill sat motionless with a stony expression. The next man up, a tall boy with a loose batting motion, struck out after missing three straight fast balls. He left the batter's box with dark looks at young Feller.

Bob, using a big, slow motion, got two strikes on the third batter. The crowd was strangely quiet watching this chunky fifteen-year-old boy pitch with the skill of a veteran.

Bob was in the middle of his windup when he heard a yell. The man on third was streaking for the plate. The first thing to flash through his mind was not to panic. He could almost hear his father's words, so patiently drilled into the boy, "Just go through your normal motion—the ball will get there first."

Bob, fighting the urge to hurry, concentrated on the pitch. He sent it low and inside so the catcher could be in a position for a quick tag. The catcher was waiting with the ball when the runner slid home into the third out.

The Oak Views rushed in to pound Bob's back wildly as though he had just won a World Series game. Blushing, Bob hid his embarrassment with a grin and ambled to the bench. He sat down next to his father.

"Good boy," Bob heard his father say and he felt the tight grasp on his arm. A warm and wonderful glow surged through the lad.

The rest of the game was a happy dream. Bob gave a few hits and a couple of walks, but no one scored. Bill used him in relief a few more times and the boy never allowed a run, but that didn't make him a pitcher yet.

Bill wasn't certain and neither was Bob, who still preferred to play short. But the Oak Views still lacked pitchers and Bill constantly was on the lookout for a pitcher. He tried out several promising boys, but they couldn't fill the job.

"For Pete's sake," one of Bill's closest baseball friends, the manager of the Valley Junction Terminals, exploded one day. "You've got a pitcher right there on your team. Your own Bob. Why look anywhere else?"

Bill frowned. "I keep thinking Bob's good enough," he said slowly, "but then maybe it's only the father in me. You know, seeing what I want to see."

"You're batty, Feller," the friend said. "Why the boy is good enough for a faster team. He's even too good for the whole league. You're leaning over too far backwards."

"Maybe you're right," Bill conceded. "Well, there's only one way to find out. I'll start him tomorrow against Waukee."

Bob was fifteen, about five-feet eight and weighed 140 pounds. He was playing against a lot older and bigger fellows and handling himself as well or better.

The Waukee experiment proved a roaring success. Bob's fast ball had the Waukee batters in a fog, as he struck out twenty-three, and Oak View pounded out a 9 to 2 victory.

Valley Junction was the Oak Views' next rival in a Sunday game. "Do us all a favor and pitch Bob," the Terminals' manager, who had convinced Bill to use his son as a hurler, now urged. "It'll boost the gate. Everyone wants to see your boy."

There were close to 2,000 fans in the packed stands for the game, all of whom departed after the Oak Views' 9 to 1 triumph discussing Bob's pitching with awed respect. He struck out twenty, gave one hit, and was touched for the lone run on an error and passed ball.

Bob Feller was becoming a baseball figure in his own corner of Iowa.

A controversial figure, in fact.

It happened in Van Meter the next day, when Bill Feller was in town to buy supplies. Walking past the barber shop, he heard his name called in a loud ringing tone.

"Feller, hey Feller."

He turned to face a stout, florid-faced man in a rumpled suit. He had a shock of tawny blond hair, mean eyes, and a brash manner that was strangely irritating to Bill.

"You the one who's got the Oak View team with the boy wonder pitcher?" the man shouted.

Bill merely nodded, disliking this flamboyant loud-mouth on sight.

"I've got the De Soto club," the man continued, neither extending his hand nor introducing himself. "How about a game next Sunday. We'd like to knock your new pitcher out of the box." He laughed raucously, and Bill felt the anger slowly travel up the back of his neck. There were echoing titters of laughter.

A small group of onlookers eager for excitement gathered around. De Soto was a fairly large community in the same part of the state. It boasted a strong ball club and a great many fervent rooters who believed their team the strongest in the state.

"We're booked this week end," Bill said quietly. "And besides, our boys don't bet on games."

"Don't get scared," the big man roared, turning to the

others with an I-told-you-so expression. "Some of your town folks here'll put up money—to lose!" The last was said with obvious scorn.

Feller heard the murmur of the crowd behind him, friends ired by the De Soto manager's insults. "Don't let him get away with that, Bill," someone said, and others voiced the same sentiment.

"Afraid to put your boy up against a real team, ain't you?" the obnoxious intruder continued. "I've seen him pitch and I'll tell you right now he won't last three innings against us. We'll eat up that fast ball."

Bill held his temper on a tight rein, but knew he was close to the breaking point. He looked the stranger in the eyes coldly. "We'll play you, Sunday." He didn't trust himself to say more.

"Yeah, but make sure your boy pitches," the visitor sneered. "Don't give us any ringer."

Bill stepped forward, then halted. No use in fighting this stupid man, he thought. Let Bob show him.

"Bob will pitch," he promised grimly, then turned and strode away before he smashed his fist into that red, ugly face.

He could still hear the jeering tone as he slammed his old car over the road home.

CHAPTER SEVEN

Bill Feller still simmered with anger when his team took the field against De Soto before a large and boisterously hostile crowd. The fans hooted and jeered as the Oak Views warmed up and they jeered Bob disgracefully.

"Papa's boy" was the mildest epithet flung at the youngster, who remained grimly impassive. If anything, the jeers made Bob more determined to show up these folks for his father's sake.

The De Soto manager stared across the diamond with a smug grin. He had padded his lineup for the game with star players from various sections to such an extent that only two De Soto regulars were still in uniform.

"They're sure out to get us," the Oak View catcher growled. "If that's the De Soto team, we're the New York Yankees."

"Look like real pros, don't they?" someone else on the Oak View bench muttered. "Big guys, too, and they're good. Boy, they sure look big."

From the bench, Feller's team watched De Soto move the ball expertly around the field in practice. Bill sat next to Bob, who had finished his warmup.

"Don't let 'em scare you," Bill said quietly to Bob. "Big or small, old or young, makes no difference if you're throwing right."

"They don't scare me, Dad," Bob answered evenly. It was the truth. He wasn't nervous. The jeering fans, the irritating De Soto manager and the imported ringers added up to a challenge which imbued young Feller with a feeling of strength and calm that amazed him.

"Just relax and pitch like you always do," his father advised. He studied Bob for a few moments, then, a slow smile creasing his face and lighting his eyes, he said, "Maybe we'll show the folks what a real pitcher looks like."

The Oak Views, as visitors, were at bat first and they went down rapidly. The De Soto pitcher was good. Bob walked out to the mound.

On sighting the small sturdy youngster, the crowd let out a roar of derision. The fans broke out with insults, catcalls, boos, screams, and foot-stamping as Bob took his warmup pitches. Then the umpire signaled for the first batter.

A broad-shouldered redhead, one of the imported stars, stepped to the plate. Bob sized him up, nodded, and began his windup. The fans increased their noise. Bob kicked his leg high, pivoted sharply on his right foot, and slammed in his first pitch.

Zing! The ball whipped across the plate in a white streak. The batter never moved a muscle. Strike one!

He swung at the next pitch, which seemed even faster. Too late. Strike two! He was out on the next delivery, another fast ball across the letters for the third strike.

Some of the hooters quieted down, but the crowd still was clamorous.

On the De Soto bench, someone asked the chastened lead-off man, "What's the kid got?"

"Speed, boy, speed—and plenty of it," he answered.

"He'll slow up," another player promised.

"Yeah, maybe," said the leadoff, now seated, "he better, or we'll never get a look at the ball."

It was a prophetic statement. Bob mowed them down like a threshing machine at harvest time. The strikeouts piled up as the innings rolled by and De Soto remained hitless. A few reached base through a walk or an error, but none went far.

Meanwhile, the Oak Views, chipping off a run here and there, entered the last half of the ninth inning ahead 2 to 0.

The crowd, now hushed, seemed awed by the spectacle of a fifteen-year-old kid throwing with such blinding speed that a team of all stars couldn't get one measly hit. Now they were rooting for Feller to end the game.

The no-hitter bubble burst in the ninth. A left-hander managed to time a fast ball for a clean hit to left field. He still was on first when Bob ended the game by striking out the De Sotos' home-run batter, for his fifteenth strikeout.

The crowd poured out of the stands to surround the new hero, the same kid they had laughed at not so long before. Even the De Soto manager came over to congratulate Bob and his father.

"Guess I was all wrong about that boy of yours," he said to Bill, extending his hand. "No hard feeling, I hope."

Bill gave him a long, level look, then shrugged and slowly offered his hand. "You never know what's in a package until you open it."

"The kid's gonna be a great pitcher some day," the De Soto

pilot went on. "I'd hate to be batting against him when he grows up."

The Oak Views were a happy bunch on the ride home, but none happier nor more pleased than Bill Feller and son.

Bob had to break away from a huge family reunion at the Feller farm the next Sunday to pitch for a Des Moines semi-pro team against Truro. Family affairs were fun, but nothing could interfere when baseball called.

There were no hoots or jeers, this time, when young Feller, whose face bore no fuzz yet, took the mound in company with men whose toughened skins had long felt the scrape of a razor.

No one shouted "Papa's boy" to the chunky pitcher, as he shut out Truro with two hits and twelve strikeouts. Beard or no beard, Feller threw too hard to laugh off.

With school out for the summer—he now attended Van Meter High—Bob signed with the Valley Junction Junior American Legion team. He had pitched several games for the school team, one in which he fanned twenty of twenty-one batters in a seven-inning contest.

Bob pitched Valley Junction to the junior state title in American Legion play and a record of seventy-nine strike-outs in forty games. The championship final against Indian-ola was played in the ball park of the professional Des Moines Western League team.

Walking on to the diamond in the Des Moines park was a new thrill for Bob. He paused for a moment to savor the sweeping curve of the stands, the well-tended grass, the beautifully marked infield—and the dugout!

It was the first time he ever had been in a dugout. Back home, the players sat on hard benches alongside the diamond. Luxuriating in a dugout was thrilling the lad more than what he did to the Indianola batters.

Valley Junction won 6 to 1 easily, with Bob hurling a one-hitter and striking out an even dozen batters. The shutout was spoiled by a lone hit and a wild throw to third.

It had been a wonderful summer for Bob. He was growing up. Baseball no longer was a catch behind the barn, a fungo session in the pasture with Dad or something to dream about at night. This was the real thing. He had arrived.

And he was a pitcher, definitely and forever. Over the summer, Bob had won ten straight games and struck out 161 batters. The Feller name was beginning to mean something in baseball around Iowa.

But the greatest moment of Bob's fifteen years came early that fall, after supper one night. He and Dad were lolling on the porch and Mom was inside getting little Marguerite off to bed.

It was a night to remember. The sky was dark velvet encrusted with millions of starry gems. A gentle breeze wafted the sweet smell of clover across the porch. They had been talking baseball until the beauty of the night pushed away all need for speech.

Bill broke the silence. The impending Detroit-St. Louis World Series had been on his mind for some time.

"How'd you like to see a big league game?" he asked softly.

Bob plopped down the legs of his propped-up chair with a bang.

"Boy, would I."

"Got any preference?"

"Sure . . . I dunno . . . Oh, any game, Dad, any game," Bob spluttered.

"Any objections to a World Series game?" Bill continued, enjoying the bewildered rapture on his son's face.

Bob was out of his chair, standing rigidly in front of his father.

"Dad." His voice rose. "You're not kidding? . . ."

Bill could tease such earnestness no longer.

"Yup, son," he said. "Figure we're due a look at the big leaguers.

"The Tigers will be in St. Louis for two games and we're gonna see 'em. You and me."

CHAPTER EIGHT

Traveling to St. Louis by auto was adventure in itself, but making the trip to see the two best teams in major league baseball battling for the world title was sheer bliss for a fifteen-year-old boy who had never been beyond Iowa.

It was just as exhilarating for Bill Feller, although he daren't admit as much to his family or friends. Some of the folks around Van Meter thought Bill was mistaken in letting Bob see big leaguers play.

"He'll be discouraged when he sees how much better real pros are," they warned. "The gap is too big between them."

Bill merely laughed their fears away. Bob was like him, Bill knew, and he always felt he had the stuff to become a big leaguer. Bob would react the same way.

They set out in the ancient car early one morning when the pink first began to streak the sky. Mom's basket lunch was stowed in the back along with a ball and gloves. That was Bob's idea.

"We'll do it up right," Bill told him the night before they left. "We're stopping at a good hotel in St. Louis."

"You mean right in the city?" Bob asked, not enthusiastic at all.

"Sure, we'll find one close to the ballpark," Bill answered.

"Well . . . where are we gonna catch?" Bob persisted.

"Catch?" The question startled Bill. "You mean to tell me —that beats me!" Bill waggled his head and rolled his eyes in mock dismay.

"Aw, Dad," Bob said sheepishly. "When I see those fellers playing . . . well, there's a lot of hints and things I figure to pick up and I want to try them out while they're still fresh."

For the first time in his life, Bill was amazed by his own son. He stared at the boy, suddenly seeing him in a new light.

There was an undeniable sincerity and purpose in Bob that came through and touched other people. It stemmed from a strong body fed by an inner faith in his own baseball destiny.

The baseball machine Bill had wrought from his own sinews and conviction was moving out from under him. Bill sensed it. There was a drive in Bob more powerful than even he had realized.

"Where do you want to stay?" Bill asked finally.

"Any tourist camp near enough to the park," Bob responded quickly. "Just so long as we get enough room to throw the ball around."

"Guess we'd look kinda silly tossing a baseball up and down a hotel lobby," mused Bill, the image evoking amusement.

So the baseball gear was stowed with the food and satchels.

St. Louis overwhelmed Bob. The busy streets, the buildings and, most of all, the enormous throngs of people impressed the boy from Van Meter.

But it was old Sportsman's Field, now gaily bedecked in flags and bunting, and the Cardinals and Tigers that made the deepest impression. Nothing else mattered.

The series stood one game apiece. Dizzy Dean, the ace of the Cardinals' pitching staff, had overwhelmed the Tigers, easily winning the series' opener in Detroit by an 8 to 3 score. The next day the Tigers' "Schoolboy" Rowe hurled Detroit to a 3 to 2 win, and now Bob was literally beside himself with excitement as Dizzy Dean's brother Paul out-pitched the great Tommy Bridges to register a 4 to 1 triumph.

Bob noted the easy pitching stance of the great Paul Dean, saw how he pitched to the great Tiger sluggers Hank Green-berg, Charley Gehringer, and Goose Goslin. Dean's master-ful hurling had the Tigers helpless, and Feller didn't miss a move. Though his main interest was the pitching of the Dean brothers, he thrilled to the sensational play of the great Pepper Martin who slammed out a triple, double and single as the crowd roared over each sensational play.

Bob's keen brown eyes studied every move on the field. When the Fellers returned to their lodgings on the city outskirts after dining out, they immediately donned their gloves and worked on the things Bob had noted during the game.

The trip was a memorable experience for Bob. He returned to the farm not only more determined than ever to make the grade as a big leaguer, but convinced he could do it.

Bob changed his stance on the mound. He altered his windup. He tinkered with his follow-through. He experi-mented. All through that winter, he and his dad worked at perfecting his pitching technique.

Bill rigged up new lights in the barn. With the chores

done, the two wasted no time getting to the business of baseball.

There were other interests to occupy a boy of sixteen now sprouting to husky manhood. Bob did not neglect his high school studies or his social life and he joined the basketball team. He wasn't much of a player, but running around kept him in shape, and the coach didn't mind having a strong back available even if he did miss shots. Bob was pretty good gathering in rebounds and could pass accurately if a bit too hard.

The Fellers went outdoors with ball and glove as soon as the frost was off the ground. They lit out for the homemade diamond and energetically went to work putting it into shape for action. Before they realized, spring and another baseball season was upon them.

Bill had agreed to manage the Farmers Union team of Des Moines, which played in top amateur competition. Bob, naturally, was the pitcher. All notions of him playing another position were gone forever.

The season opened with a rush for the Fellers. Hurling against the Slater, Iowa, team in May, Bob pitched a 2 to 1 victory on three hits and seventeen strikeouts.

Next, Bob shut out the crack Yale, Iowa, town team 5 to 0 on a no-hitter with twenty-two strikeouts! The baseball grapevine was humming. Now the big league scouts were getting reports of a sensational farm youngster in Iowa who was reported to be faster than the great Walter Johnson.

It was after Bob shut out St. Mary's 1 to 0 in a three-hitter with nineteen more strikeouts, that the Fellers had a visitor on their farm one sweltering day late in July.

Bob was driving the tractor on the wheat combine when

he first spotted a man picking his way through the field. As the figure drew closer, Bob saw that he was tall and thin, wore a light, rumpled suit, and was perspiring profusely.

Bob stopped the tractor and his dad looked up, noticing the stranger for the first time.

"Howdedo," the man said, extending his hand. "I'm Cyril Slapnicka."

Bill nodded, shook hands, but seemed unimpressed by that name.

"Of the Cleveland Indians," Slapnicka continued.

Bill's interest perked up, and Bob's heart almost ceased beating.

"This the young pitcher I've been hearing about?" the visitor asked, nodding toward Bob.

"That's him," Bill said. "What brings you out here?"

"I'm an Iowa man, myself," Slapnicka explained. "Cedar Rapids. I wanted to see your boy pitch. When's his next game?"

"He goes Sunday in Des Moines for the Farmers Union team," Bill answered.

"Couple of other boys I want to look at it," Slapnicka went on in a brisk, businesslike manner. Then he turned to Bob with a pleasant smile.

"You look like a pretty strong lad," he said. "Baseball's more fun than farming, isn't it?"

Bob gulped and choked out a muttered yes.

Slapnicka smiled. He had met so many embarrassed, wide-eyed youngsters. The magic of the name—Cleveland Indians!

He turned back to Bill, shook hands again, wished Bob luck, and made his way through the field.

Bob felt numb with shock. This was the big leagues beckoning. Just as casually as that. A thin stranger comes out of the shimmering heat to open the door . . . Bob was yanked back to reality with his father's words: "Let's get back to work, Son."

Bob was nervous before the game, Sunday. He kept peering around for Slapnicka, but never did manage to spot that elusive gentleman. Wherever he hid, Slapnicka was there and saw enough to bring him out to the Feller home that very night.

Bob wasn't in the room while the Cleveland representative and his father discussed his baseball future. After Slapnicka left, Bob learned that his father had signed him to play for Fargo-Moorehead of the Northern League in North Dakota. It was a Cleveland minor league farm club.

"Don't talk about it," Bill Feller told his son. "It might sound like bragging. Or maybe make some of the others jealous . . ."

Buoyed by the knowledge that he, sixteen-year-old Bob Feller, was part of a big league organization, the youngster poured it on ever harder after that. He fanned twenty-two and gave only three hits against Bennett, then whiffed twenty-three against an Iowa all-star team before 10,000 spectators at Tipton, Iowa.

His father seemed strangely saddened after the game. They were leaving the park when Bill said, "I won't be managing you much longer. Next summer you'll be playing for other folks."

A sudden sense of apprehension filled Bob. He had never thought about being separated from his dad. They had been with each other ever since he could remember.

It was a moment of strange and inexplicable anguish for

the boy. He couldn't think of anything to say to brighten his dad's mood. They drove home in uncomfortable silence, the day's triumph forgotten in the unspoken despair of a father facing the inexorable march of time that makes his boy into a man and takes him away.

CHAPTER NINE

Bill Feller tried not to dwell on his son's eventual departure, of which he was as certain as the fact the wheat he grew would be converted into foodstuffs.

Bob was on the verge of manhood, Bill rationalized, and would have to step out on his own sooner or later. A father's job is to prepare his children to stand on their own feet, and Bob was prepared to do his job well.

There still was a wide gap between signing a contract and pitching in the major leagues. Bill knew there were some important local assignments waiting for Bob in the immediate days ahead.

Foremost was winning the sectional tournament to qualify for the national semi-pro championships scheduled for Dayton, Ohio, in September. To get there, the Farmers Union team would have to beat Iowa's best at the annual state fair.

Bill emerged from his team's 10 to 7 victory in the opener at the Iowa fair, bathed in perspiration and shaken by the game. Although Bob fanned eighteen and gave only three hits, his wildness kept him in constant trouble.

Bob was pitching hard, but he wasn't always aiming the

ball too well. As all pitchers learn, the strike zone narrows considerably against good batters and Bob was confronting stronger opposition each time out.

In addition to wildness Bob encountered catcher troubles. None of his receivers could handle Bob's speed. In one game six batters who swung at third strikes made first base safely because the catchers couldn't hold on to the ball.

Not that it made any difference in this tournament, Bill reflected as he trudged off the diamond. Farmers Union was finished and everyone knew it. The Iowa final was tomorrow and Bob couldn't be expected to pitch two days in a row. Without Bob on the hill—impossible.

The morning of the game, Bob approached his father.

"Let me pitch today," he begged. "Honest, I'm not tired a bit. I feel great. I can do it."

Bill shook his head.

"Nothing doing," he said. Desperate as he was for a pitcher, the risk was too great. "You might ruin your arm—for good."

"Dad, I tell you I can do it," the boy insisted.

"No, you'd have to bear down all the way against this club and I won't take the chance."

"Dad, listen to me, please," Bob pleaded. "Did I ever have a sore arm? Did I?"

Bill said nothing, merely looking at him.

"I've pitched to you for hours and hours, day after day, and never hurt my arm."

Bob's insistence surprised the older man. It was something new in the boy. Maybe this was the time to find out what Bob had, Bill thought. Get it over with, once and for all.

54

Sensing his father weakening, Bob renewed his argument. "Dad," he said, "if I'm off, we'll both know it soon enough and you can yank me. There's no harm in trying. We'll surely get murdered the other way."

Bill yielded with a fatalistic shrug.

"All right," he said. "It's up to you. Just promise me one thing. Don't punish the arm. The slightest twinge or weakness—stop!"

Bob assented, happily.

"Remember that promise," his father warned again. "That right arm is your whole career."

Then he gave Bob a slow wink and the tight little grin that was so much a part of him. "Let's win it," he said, lightly punching Bob's arm with the side of his fist.

Win it he did. Bob's bat was as important as his arm in the triumph. He got three hits, his last driving in the winning run. The other team got only four hits and struck out thirteen times. Bob's control was unsteady, but his opponents were so demoralized by his blazing speed, they never did see what they were swinging at.

"How is the arm?" Bill asked anxiously, after the game.

"I could go nine more," Bob answered seriously. It hadn't bothered him and he hadn't thought about it. "How'd you like that hitting?" he bubbled, showing his teeth in a wide grin.

"You got Hornsby scared stiff," Bill chuckled.

The trip to Dayton was an exciting event for the entire community. The team was given a gala send-off. For each player, it was the golden opportunity to perform before an avalanche of big league scouts assembled to size up their capabilities.

The Farmers Union opponent was a team from Battle Creek, Michigan. Bob went to the mound feeling strong enough to hurl the ball through a brick wall. He struck out eighteen batters and gave two hits, but lost 1 to 0 when his center fielder dropped an easy fly to let in the lone run.

The defeat could not obscure young Feller's brilliance as a pitcher. The big league scouts clustered around Bill like flies. He didn't have a free moment from then until he left Dayton, two days later.

The questing scouts meant nothing to Bob, heartbroken by the loss. Farmers Union had one more chance to stay in the tourney. It would have to win the next day—without Bob pitching. Bill was adamant on that point. Bob pleaded in vain for a chance to pitch.

The team lost, and the disappointed Fellers and their friends returned home.

It had been a fruitful trip. The baseball world, or that portion of it which dealt with the search for young prospects, was well aware of a phenomenal right-hander named Bob Feller who threw thunderbolts.

It was to learn a great deal more about him in the space of one year.

CHAPTER TEN

Bob had been signed by the Indians, but no word was given to the press. Not even the Cleveland scouts at Dayton were aware the young ace was under contract to them.

Bill Bradley and Buzz Wetzel, scouting for the Indians, pursued Bob as strenuously as did the others. Frank Rickey was there for the St. Louis Cardinals, Pat Monohan for the St. Louis Browns, Bill Doyle and Steve O'Rourke for the Detroit Tigers, and Fred Hunter for the Boston Red Sox.

Bill was besieged with dazzling offers, enough possibly to have made him wonder if he hadn't acted too hastily in accepting Slapnicka's terms. O'Rourke offered Feller $9,000 for his son's signature and threw in an all expenses paid trip for the entire family to the World Series. He even promised to have Bob's tonsils and adenoids removed free!

Hunter phoned Eddie Collins in Boston to come west with a huge amount of money. He wanted to bundle the Fellers off on an auto trip and get them away from the other scouts. But Bill merely sat and listened, unable to do anything about the offers.

For Bob, with summer and the baseball season over, life returned to the normal routine. A junior at Van Meter High

School, he reported to the basketball coach again. This year, six feet tall and weighing over 175 pounds, Bob won a starting berth as center.

Sometime between then and the spring of 1936, Bob hurt his pitching arm. It may have been on the basketball court, where Bob relied more on rough strength than finesse, or in the spring plowing. The tractor turned balky one day, and Bob felt an awful wrench in his shoulder.

When he tried to pitch, a sharp pain stabbed him through the shoulder; he winced visibly on his first throw and dropped to his knees. Bill rushed over to the boy.

"What is it?" he cried.

Bob clutched the aching shoulder with his left hand. He grimaced in pain. "I can't throw," he said haltingly. "It hurts like the blazes. Oh, Dad. It hurts so much."

Bill wrote to Slapnicka that night. Slapnicka wired back in a few days, informing Bill to avoid pitching and do nothing until they heard from him.

It was spring, the school baseball season had begun, and Bob Feller was only seventeen years old. It was torture to watch games from the sidelines. Beyond that, there was the haunting fear that he may have seriously hurt himself.

Spurred by Bill's anxious notes, Slapnicka finally asked Bob to report to Cleveland as soon as the school term was finished. The summons revived the unhappy boy like a spring tonic.

The day Bob left was warm and mild. The fields were green and the land bursting with life. Mom was packing Bob's clothes when his dad signaled.

"Let's take a walk," Bill suggested.

They strolled in silence, occupied with bittersweet

thoughts. They strode across the fields to the old diamond Bill and he had built.

"It won't look like much after you see those big league parks," Bill said, a strange, wry smile tugging at his mouth. "But I'll always love it."

Bob couldn't look at his dad. "So will I," he choked.

At the train, parting was an agonizing wrench again. Bob kissed his mother and sister Marguerite, shook hands solemnly with his father.

"You'll make it," Bill said, pride overcoming the pain of departure. Both understood what he meant. Bob gripped his dad's hand tighter, then turned and went up the train steps.

Being on his own, facing the greatest adventure in the seventeen years of his life, was too exciting for Bob to dwell long on sad thoughts. His mind raced ahead to Cleveland, concocting glorious daydreams in which he won pennants and world series.

The size and bustle of Cleveland threw a momentary scare into the big farm boy at first. Then, remembering his dad's advice on handling any tough situation, Bob sailed into it.

He found the Indians' Old League Park and was directed to the executive offices.

Bob wore a rumpled brown suit of obvious country cut and slightly tight at the seams. His hair, cut long, flopped behind his ears. His full, round, smooth face mingled innocence and wariness. He carried two bulging old leather valises.

Slapnicka, gazing up from his desk, regarded the boy blankly for a moment. Then his eyes lit in recognition and he came out of his seat with a smile. He understood the boy's feeling of awkwardness and loneliness and tried to put him at ease.

"Leave your things here," Slapnicka said. "Come with me. I'll show you around."

They walked through the office and under the stands onto the field.

It was a miracle cure. Bob gawked at the empty stands, stretching away for what seemed miles and miles. The sun was bright and hot, the grass a thick, lush carpet of green, such as he never had trod on before.

It was the first time he had ever been on a big league diamond. Slapnicka was silent as they walked around the field. Bob forgot his strangeness and his discomfort.

They went out to the mound. Bob looked first toward home plate, imagining a catcher squatting behind the plate. Then he turned slowly, his eyes wandering to the fences.

Bob's eyes were shining and his face glowing. Slapnicka regarding the boy through kindly eyes, envied this wonderful gift of freshness with which youth saw everything.

Bob's gaze halted suddenly at the right field fence. A slight frown clouded his face. This is interesting, Slapnicka thought, the kid knows his baseball!

"Kind of close," Bob remarked. The fence was only 290 feet down the right-field line.

"Not so bad," Slapnicka smiled, "when you learn how to handle it. Just be careful with lefty batters. The main thing is to get that arm of yours right again."

They went under the stands again into the Cleveland dressing room. Again Bob gawked, noting the names on the lockers . . . names he had heard and read about . . . Hal

Trosky . . . Earl Averill . . . Mel Harder . . . Johnny Allen
. . . Sammy Hale . . .

The room was empty now. The Indians were on the road.

"This is where you'll dress," Slapnicka said, a bit more
briskly now that the youngster seemed to be over his fright.

"Come, Bob," Slapnicka continued, smiling again at the
awestruck youngster's reluctance to leave. "We've got to get
you a decent place to live. And there's someone I want you
to meet."

It was Bruce Campbell, a regular right fielder who had
suffered an attack of spinal meningitis and had been left
behind to recuperate. Bruce, a strapping man with a genial
disposition, worked out every day and was recovering nicely.

Bob shook hands with Bruce, as Slapnicka told them they
could work out on the field together every day.

"Just take it very easy," the Cleveland official instructed
Feller. "Loosen up. That's about all. When the club gets
back, we'll have Lefty look at the shoulder."

He referred to Max (Lefty) Weisman, the trainer, who
knew almost everything there is to know about baseball ail-
ments.

"You're a big feller," Bruce quipped when they met the
next day. Bob weighed about 185 now and stood a fraction
over six feet tall. He was built hard and solid, with a hint of
great strength in wide shoulders and heavy neck muscles.

"Throw a real hard one, I bet," Bruce said.

Bob shrugged modestly. A raw kid doesn't brag about
his speed to a major leaguer. "All I hope I can do now is
throw," he said in a worried tone.

"Heck, we two sick ones will get well together," Campbell

laughed. "C'mon now, let's get out in the sun. Nature's remedy."

They threw back and forth to each other every day, ran around a lot and gradually Bob felt the shoulder loosening up. Once in a while, Slapnicka, a former minor league pitcher himself, would emerge from his office and instruct Bob. Sometimes he even would get behind the plate and catch Bob. "Looks better every day, Bob. You're doing fine."

No question about it now. The arm and shoulder were stronger. Bruce had to warn Bob repeatedly about throwing easier. "I'm no catcher," he'd shout. "Have a heart. I'm a sick outfielder, just trying to help out."

The first person Bob met when the Indians returned from the east was trainer Lefty Weisman. "Take care of this boy's arm," Slapnicka said, and from that day on, the capable trainer looked after Feller like a big brother.

"Hop on," Lefty told Bob with a broad wink, motioning to the rubbing table. Lefty had come a long way to Cleveland, leaving a newsboy job in Boston to follow Tris Speaker, his boyhood baseball hero. Speaker got him a job, around the clubhouse. Lefty did everything, learned everything, and now was considered one of the ablest trainers and conditioners in the game.

He studied Bob's arm, poked it, kneaded it, twisted it, then pronounced: "Nothing serious. You'll be throwing as hard as ever in a couple of weeks."

The ruby-faced trainer was as good as his word. It wasn't long before Bob could bear down with every ounce of power without feeling a twinge.

It didn't escape Slapnicka, who called Feller aside one

day, "No sense just warming up here every day," he said. "How would you like to play?"

The startled look on Bob's round face amused the older man. "No, not with the Indians—yet!" he added. "There's a good local team here called the Rosenblums. You can pitch for them. Suit you?"

"Yes, sir, Mr. Slapnicka," Bob responded eagerly. It was fun hanging around the stadium close to the big leaguers, all of whom treated him cordially, but the inactivity bored him.

The Cleveland Rosenblums, a semi-pro outfit representing a large clothing store, played in what amounted to Class C company.

Bob was surprised to see Slapnicka present at Woodland Hills Park, a local public diamond, for his first start against a team of stars from Akron. He was even more surprised to notice a photographer from one of the Cleveland newspapers covering the game.

It was a great day for Bob. He struck out fifteen batters, and then won the game in the tenth inning with a line drive single to left that gave his team a 3 to 2 margin.

Slapnicka was beaming when he came over to congratulate Bob. "Good pitching, son," he said. "Maybe we ought to get you something tougher. How would that be?" He was smiling broadly.

"Anything you say, Mr. Slapnicka," Bob answered, puzzled at the older man's expression.

"Fine," Slapnicka snapped. "How about the St. Louis Cardinals?"

The Cards' Gas House Gang were the rollicking, roaring bunch he had seen whip Detroit in the 1934 World Series.

They had such awesome players as Dizzy Dean and his brother Paul, Pepper Martin, Joe Medwick, Terry Moore, Leo Durocher, and were managed by Frankie Frisch.

It was preposterous, of course, but Bob would go along with a joke. "Sure," he grinned back. "When do we start?"

"July sixth," Slapnicka answered seriously. "They'll be in here for an exhibition game with us and I think it would —" He paused, noticing Bob's gaping expression. "Now don't worry," he laughed. "I wouldn't put you in there if I didn't think it would do you good."

Don't worry, Bob said to himself! Don't worry! That was about all he could do until the fateful day.

CHAPTER ELEVEN

Bob rose earlier than usual the morning of the game with the Cardinals. It was still gray outside, and he tried to fall asleep again by curling under the light blanket.

It was useless. He was too excited by what the day promised. Not really nervous or even jumpy, but extremely wide awake. Sleep was impossible.

It's so dark out, he thought—maybe it might rain! He leaped to the window. No, it would be a clear beautiful day, he saw, ashamed of his thought.

No sense fretting, he reasoned after a while, remembering his father's words. "Makes no difference who's batting," Dad always drawled, "just so long as you can throw the ball past him."

The mental picture was comforting, and Bob felt himself relax. That queasy, empty feeling in the pit of his stomach, he knew, could be cured at the breakfast table.

Feller reached the ball park early, but not before Lefty Weisman or Steve O'Neill, the Cleveland manager. Steve, a stubby, genial man who had been a star catcher for the Indians, knew baseball and understood people.

"How's the arm?" he asked cheerfully, his tone warm and

encouraging. "Let's show these Cards a thing or two today."

Bob gave him a wan smile. "I sure hope so," he said.

"Attaboy," O'Neill continued. "I'll catch you myself and we'll work the middle three innings."

On the way to the field, Bob bumped into Slapnicka.

"You look big league, Bob," he said. "Just keep throwing the way you've been and there's nothing to worry about." He sent Bob on his way with a pat.

The park was half full, about 12,000 fans in the stands. The Cards started most of their regulars—Medwick, Moore, and Martin in the outfield, Leo Durocher and Collins in the infield with Gelbert and Garibaldi, Ogrodowski behind the plate, and Munns, a young pitcher on the mound.

Bob didn't see much of the first three innings. He loosened up in the bullpen as George Uhle, a fine right-hander now past his prime and employed as a coach, hurled. The game was tied at 1 to 1 when Bob got the call.

The sweat poured down his face and body, but Bob felt ice cold walking to the mound. The crowd was a blur and his breathing not too steady.

Then he noticed Steve's wide face grinning at him.

"Ready, kid?" he beamed. Bob nodded, his eyes narrowed in concentration, his mouth a tight determined line.

Thank God, O'Neill thought, the kid isn't going into a funk. He's got guts, the manager decided. "Just give 'em the fast ball," he said, slowly. "No curve, nothing fancy. I'll give signals just to make it look good, but all you do is let it rip."

O'Neill's confidence was heartening. He grinned, flipped the ball to Bob, and headed back to the plate.

Bob felt all alone on the mound with 12,000 pairs of eyes

66

focused on him. He gripped the ball hard, as if to squeeze reassurance out of it. He drew in a deep, long breath as O'Neill braced himself for the warmup pitches.

Self-consciousness made Bob stiff and unsure in his first few tosses. He sneaked a glance at the St. Louis dugout. None of the Cards even seemed interested to look at him. Their indifference annoyed him. Did they think he was such a dud? Angrily, Bob fired the last warmup in emphatically.

There was a slight stir in the crowd as Bruce Ogrodowski walked to the plate, carelessly swinging two bats. He tossed one aside, settled into the box, and studied the young stranger on the mound.

Bob took a long, slow windup, his left leg high, his body back. Then he let loose. The ball leaped across the plate like a cobra, snaking into O'Neill's mitt with a sharp smack.

"Strike!" the umpire shouted, his arm raised.

O'Neill grinned.

"See that one?" he murmured to the startled batter.

The next pitch was a ball, inside, but even faster than the other. Ogrodowski moved back slightly, on his toes and ready to duck. He went for the next one, still swinging when the ball thudded into the mitt.

"Lemme out here in one piece," Ogrodowski muttered to the chuckling backstop. He got his wish quickly, going out on a bunt try that bounded into the third baseman's hands.

Leo Durocher strode to the plate. Leo the Lip, a fresh guy who knew all the angles and never gave an inch. "C'mon plowboy," he shouted. "Let's see how you pitch hay back home on the farm."

It didn't bother Bob. He felt calm now, sure of himself

and the power in his right arm. He reared back and fogged three strikes past Durocher, who swung gamely if ineffectively. Leo swaggered back to the dugout, waggling his fingers like a man who had been scorched standing too close to the flame.

Feller pumped three more strikes past Art Garibaldi, the last one well outside but so smoky fast the poor second-stringer didn't see it until too late.

Bob lumbered back to his dugout, chest thrust out, head up, foot forward. It was a plowboy gait, a farmer's walk, and the sharp-eyed bench jockeys caught it immediately.

He sat down next to O'Neill. "You're killing 'em, kid," Steve said. "I just hope you don't kill me." Then, noticing Bob's expression, he added, "I can't move as fast as I used to."

The Indians picked up a run and led 2 to 1 when Feller returned to the mound. Munns, the pitcher, was an easy strikeout victim.

This is the way to do it, Bob thought. No trouble if you strike 'em out. Terry Moore jolted the theory with a hard single to left field. Shaken, Bob walked Stu Martin.

Bob was disgusted with himself. He stared grimly at Pepper Martin, waiting truculently at the plate.

Bob concentrated carefully as he wound up slowly and purposefully. He was halfway back when he heard a shout and caught a flashing glimpse of a figure fleeing down the basepaths. It was Moore going for third. Behind him, he heard Martin tearing for second. A double steal!

Frantically, Bob pitched. The ball sailed wide, glancing off O'Neill's mitt. Moore strode home with a wicked grin and Martin was parked on third.

It was a terrible moment for the young man fresh off the farm. He wallowed in embarrassment. Thoughts of his father's disappointment and his own shame at panicking stabbed him like knives.

To O'Neill, the inevitable had happened. This raw young chucker with his big motion and lack of experience was a sucker for smart base runners. Compassion welled in him for the poor kid's suffering.

"Don't let it get you," Steve said lamely to Bob. "It's not your fault. Now, get out there and pitch."

Pepper Martin was a dangerous hitter and a terror on the basepaths. Bob knew what would happen if the Wild Horse of the Osage reached base. He had to get him out!

Bob never threw harder in his life. Three strikes blazed past Pepper, who went down swinging almost half-heartedly for him. Pepper wasn't digging in at the plate against this moonfaced kid who threw thunderbolts.

"I feel a lot safer in here," the St. Louis ace told his teammates in the dugout. Rip Collins felt the same way. He went out on strikes, too, missing the last bullet by a foot.

The crowd applauded Bob when he came out for his last inning.

O'Neill remained on the bench. His hand was raw and swollen from Bob's pitches. "We'll give you a spry young catcher," he told Feller with a warm smile. "Guess I'm not as young as I used to be."

Joe Becker went in to catch. He was a lanky man with quick reflexes. Feller felt like a veteran now, calm and confident, particularly with the three weak batters coming up.

But Ogrodowski fooled him with a lucky blooper down the right field line for a double. Durocher, still quipping but mighty respectful of the kid's speed, missed three in a row. After his last swing, Leo turned to Becker and said, "By George, this kid stuffs the ball down your throat."

Bob fanned Gelbert, who wasn't any more anxious than the others to face Feller's cannon delivery, and Munns went down one-two-three the same way. The inning was over. Feller had made his debut. He was confused, relieved that it was over, yet sorry to leave.

Bob still was in a daze when a photographer came running over. "C'mere, kid," he yelled. "Let's get you over here with Dizzy Dean."

Dizzy Dean! Bob still didn't believe it, even when he was standing in front of the great Cardinal flinger.

"Hey, Diz," the photographer shouted, "can I get you for a shot with this kid?"

Dizzy, a great big grin creasing his features, rose slowly. "If it's all right with him," he said. "That was some mighty fine pitching, young man." Diz offered his hand and Bob grabbed it like any hero-worshiping fan.

Bob had finished showering when the Indians came. They had won 7 to 6 and were jubilantly noisy.

"Nice going, kid," Hal Trosky said. "Glad you weren't throwing against us."

Bruce Campbell gave him a hearty whack on the shoulders. "Told you we'd both get well, didn't I?" he gloated.

Bob glowed. Lefty Weisman, the trainer, who had taken a liking to him, came over. "Better let me take care of that arm," he said. "It's pretty valuable to you and to us."

At last, Bob felt that he belonged.

CHAPTER TWELVE

Eight strikeouts in three innings against the mighty Gas House Gang, even in an exhibition game, turned the spotlight on the seventeen-year-old hurler.

While the Cleveland papers didn't go wild about Feller, the league in which he played for the Rosenblums did. The other so-called amateur teams wanted him out. Slapnicka, attempting to pour oil on troubled waters, claimed Feller wasn't being paid, but the furor did not subside.

Finally the Cleveland management came to a difficult decision, but not before Bob pitched once more for the Rosenblums, losing 3 to 2, but fanning fifteen batters before a crowd of close to 20,000. The Feller name obviously was a gate magnet already.

Slapnicka foresaw greater woes than the protests of a semi-pro league. He transferred Bob's contract from Fargo-Moorehead to the Indians' Southern Association team in New Orleans.

On July 14, Slapnicka summoned Feller to his office.

"We've formally added you to the roster," he said. Bob gazed at him blankly. "That means you're on the team now," he explained.

A major leaguer! Bob could hear the words, but wasn't sure whether he was awake or dreaming. He heard Slapnicka's voice making sounds somewhere far away.

"You need experience and by rights should get it down in New Orleans," the Cleveland general manager continued, wondering how much was registering with the star-struck youngster. "But we've decided to keep you here to work with the best men available."

Bob still hadn't uttered a word. He murmured his thanks and left the office beset by a hundred jumbled thoughts. He was leaving with the team for Philadelphia that night, worrying about the train trip, his baggage, clothing, about wiring the news to his father . . .

Slapnicka was worried, too, but not about a train ride. There were rumblings around the league at the way Feller had been signed. Whatever the trouble, he thought, Feller was worth it. Slapnicka was sure of that.

It was Bob's first Pullman trip and he was excited, although it didn't show on his placid face. It was awkward undressing in the Pullman berth and Bob was sure he'd spend an uncomfortable night. But he had ample room and quickly fell asleep to the rattle and click of the train speeding eastward over the rails.

The bright sunlight of Philadelphia, streaming through the train window, awakened him the next morning. Bob dressed hurriedly, fearful of being last, then felt restless waiting alone for an hour while the others slept.

The Indians stopped at the Benjamin Franklin Hotel, a fine old hostelry in the Quaker City, and Bob roomed with Wally Schang, the old Yankee catcher. Wally was an amiable veteran who knew all the players, their foibles, baseball strengths and weaknesses.

He enjoyed talking, and Bob enjoyed listening, especially when Wally discussed the league's great hitters. Schang spoke with engaging familiarity of Babe Ruth, Hank Greenberg, Lou Gehrig and Jimmy Foxx.

Bob felt glaringly green in the visitor's dressing room at Shibe Park. A few Indians greeted him, but Lefty Weisman made him feel at home immediately.

"I've got something for you, Bob," Lefty said with a grin. Pointing to a locker in back of the room, he said, "Try it on."

There, hanging in neat folds, was his Cleveland uniform. Putting it on gave him a strange feeling, almost like the day his dad brought home his first baseball outfit when Bob was nine years old.

The uniform was a little tight in the seat and around the chest, but sneaking occasional glances in the full length mirror near the door, Bob decided it looked great. He put on the cap. It felt big.

He didn't want to appear foolish posing in the mirror, but gathering his courage, Bob finally strode to the mirror and looked at himself. No one seemed to notice but the trainer, who was smiling broadly.

"How's it feel?" Lefty asked.

"The cap's big," Bob said.

"Keep it that way," Lefty said, with a world of wisdom in his tone. The remark wasn't lost on young Feller. It was sound advice from a man who had seen too many come and go in the harsh world of professional baseball.

Shibe Park surprised the rookie. It was much larger than the Cleveland home park. Self-conscious in his uniform, unfamiliar with the field, Bob went out on the field uncertainly.

Like a fan, he gawked at the Philadelphia players trooping back to their dugout after practice.

"Hey, Bob," he heard someone shout. It was O'Neill, ambling over. "Go on out there and shag some flies with the pitchers," he said. "You're one of the gang now."

Living with big leaguers, mingling with them in the diamond, viewing games from the dugout, listening to the same locker room gab, was a thrill and an education. It whetted Bob's determination to absorb everything, to learn everything, and to make the grade.

Old Wally was a great help. He sat with Bob during games, diagnosing the batters and the pitchers, explaining what they did and why.

The Indians swept the three-game series in Philadelphia, behind fine pitching by Mel Harder, Johnny Allen, and Denny Galehouse.

The next stop was Washington and Bob rubbernecked in the capital like any other tourist, when he wasn't at Griffith Stadium. The Indians had run up a string of seven straight wins before adding the eighth in their opener against the Senators.

They won the first game of a Sunday double-header easily, for number nine. Bob was growing bench weary, anxious to play but without hope O'Neill would use him while the Cleveland club was on a streak.

But the Senators hammered Blaeholder in the nightcap for a 5 to 2 lead by the sixth inning and increased it to 6 to 2 against Allen, when O'Neill suddenly signaled to Bob. "Go out to the bullpen," he nodded, "and warm up. You may as well get a little action."

For the first time in his life, Bob felt his nerve go. His knees wobbled and his heart pounded so fast he thought it might hammer through his chest. He managed to keep the ball in the park in his warmup and was feeling steadier when the call came.

He was going into the game! He walked in a fog of sound and white haze. He didn't hear a thing Billy Sullivan, his catcher, said. Vaguely he tried to recall the tips Schang had briefed him on the Washington batters coming up.

The tension eased as Bob warmed up, but there was a tight band across his stomach and his mouth was dry as flannel. Beads of sweat broke out like giant goose pimples when the umpire called for play.

The inning was a babble of sound and action. Nothing registered properly in his distorted senses. All he knew was to wind up and throw as hard as possible. He struck out one Senator, walked another, and was horrified watching one ball slam into Red Kress's side.

The Senators went hitless, but that wasn't Feller's fault. Washington won the game 9 to 5, and Bobby showered in glum silence. He had no taste for food at dinner time, plagued by a sense of acute humiliation.

On the train heading back to Cleveland that night, O'Neill plopped down next to the unhappy youth, who looked at him with such humble contrition that the manager had to laugh.

"Bob," he said kindly, "I'm not going to fill you full of corn about how great or how bad you looked out there today. You were wild and you were panicky."

Bob lowered his eyes, shame flaming on his cheeks.

"On the other hand," O'Neill continued, "that was a pretty

tough chore for a young lad. None of the men out there to-day broke right into big league ball his first day."

O'Neill sat silent for a while, puffing his cigar. Bob had time to reflect on the pilot's words. "I just didn't know what was going on today," Bob finally blurted. "I went yellow."

"No, no," O'Neill said. "Two things I know you've got, Bob—guts and an arm. You just blanked out. Next time it'll be a lot easier. Wait and see."

"There will be a next time?" Bob asked, with such boyish wonder and relief Steve couldn't repress a smile.

"Kid, you'll have plenty of next times," he confided, "and plenty to be proud of."

O'Neill stayed for a while, reciting some baseball experiences, telling some of the things he knew about other ball-players, until Bob completely forgot his own woes.

When the manager left, Bob's emotions had shifted gears into high again. Life was worth living and the future a storehouse of gleaming baubles.

CHAPTER THIRTEEN

Cleveland was in a turmoil over the Tribe when it returned home and Bob drifted in the aura of excitement and fervor surrounding the team.

The Indians were on a victory streak, slowly reducing the Yankees' huge lead until the Bombers led by 7½ games the day they came into town for what the sports writers call a crucial series.

Bob pitched two innings against the Athletics a week previous to the Yankee invasion, yielding three hits, walking two, and giving up one run. This time, at least, Bob wasn't so jittery, although he hit two batters. His reputation for blinding speed and wildness had spread around the league. Batters didn't take a firm toehold against Feller. They had to be prepared to duck—fast!

The Yankees lived up to everything the boy from Van Meter had heard of them. He gazed with awe at Lou Gehrig, Joe DiMaggio, Tony Lazzeri, Bill Dickey, Red Rolfe, and Frank Crosetti. He studied their great pitchers—Lefty Gomez, Red Ruffing, and Johnny Murphy.

The Bombers smashed the Indians with their war clubs for two straight victories. The third game was moved into huge Municipal Stadium, and a crowd of 65,000 poured out for it.

Slapnicka arranged for a series of field events before the game in which players from both teams would compete. To his amazement, Bob discovered he was entered in an accuracy throwing contest. The objective was to throw the ball from the pitcher's box through a paper-covered frame at home plate.

"They sure picked the right guy for this," Bob muttered to Schang. The fans, aware of his wildness, felt the same way. They burst into laughter when Feller's name was announced.

It seemed silly and, to a boy reared as rigorously in baseball as Bob, a bit undignified. But if this was what you had to do in the majors . . . well, Bob would do it.

Taking a short windup, Bob threw the first ball. It tore through the paper, close to the frame but scored as a hit. Quickly and easily, he whipped the ball dead through the center on his next four tosses.

The delighted fans gave him a loud cheer and, equally satisfying, the management rewarded him with first prize of $25. Bob only grinned wider when one loud-voiced rooter shouted, "Hey, Bobby, you hit those hoops like they was batters."

The game, a sixteen-inning thriller, ended in a 1 to 1 tie on account of darkness, a tremendous disappointment to the Indians. It left them 9½ games behind the New Yorkers in the American League pennant race.

Day by day, Bob grew more accustomed to big league ways. He roomed with Roy Weatherly, a hard-hitting Texan, who was almost as innocent of baseball experience as Bob.

He worked daily with Schang, and O'Neill made sure to watch and correct Bob at every practice.

It was a happy life in a way for Bob, but palling for a boy imbued with such eagerness to play. Bob realized he could learn only a limited amount merely watching and working out. To advance, he needed game experience.

It came quicker than he imagined. Unknown to Bob, O'Neill and Slapnicka had arrived at a decision. Steve told him about it in the clubhouse.

"I'm letting you start tomorrow," Steve said. The St. Louis Browns, managed by Rogers Hornsby, were in. "I wouldn't okay it if I didn't believe you were ready and can win it."

Bob gulped before he spoke. "I won't let you down," he promised. Studying Bob's strong, solemn face, O'Neill was sure he wouldn't.

"This is a right-handed team mostly," the manager resumed, "and I don't think they'll be crowding the plate." Both grinned at that. "The Greek will catch."

The Greek was Charles George, a rookie from New Orleans, added to the club when Frank Pytlak's jaw was broken by a Monte Pearson pitch during the Yankee series. The Greek had never started a game either, but he and Bob felt an understandable kinship. Both youngsters and new to the club, they were more comfortable with each other than with the older players.

The game was on Sunday, August 23, an oven-hot day under a blazing sun. A reporter, escaping the sun in the dugout before game time, asked Steve if pitching Feller meant he was giving up on the pennant.

"Not a bit," O'Neill answered promptly. "It's just the other way around." He paused to let this sink in. The reporter gaped at Steve in astonishment.

"Stop kidding, Steve," the newsman scoffed.

"Yeah," O'Neill said, "come on around and tell me that *after* the game." When Steve left, the reporter turned to one of the players and said, "Phew! The heat must be getting Steve."

Schang warmed Feller up in front of the stands before the game. Bob was loose and strong. The ball exploded into Wally's mitt, the crack of horsehide on leather drawing gasps from the crowd.

"Mostly fast ball," the Greek told Bob, just before the game started. "Curve once in a while. Okay, boy, let's get 'em."

Lyn Lary, first man up for the Browns, was out on three straight strikes burned right through the middle. Harland Clift got a scratch hit over the second baseman's head, but Julie Solters and Bob Bell fanned to end the inning.

It went that way for five innings, the strikeouts piling up. The ball was moving for Bob. He never had better control. But Earl Caldwell, pitching for St. Louis, had the Indians stopped cold.

With one out in the sixth, Lary doubled to center and scored on Bell's two bagger to right. Without change of expression and in an icy calm despite the withering heat, Feller struck out Sam West and Jim Bottomley, the Brown's two toughest hitters.

The Tribe retaliated with three runs off Caldwell in their half of the sixth, the big blow a double by Hal Trosky, a fellow Iowan who took a shine to Bob.

The strikeouts were piling up fast for Feller. He had twelve after six innings. "All he needs is two an inning," someone mentioned to O'Neill, who shushed him immediately. The American League record was sixteen, set by Rube Waddell in 1908, while Dizzy Dean's seventeen was the major league mark.

"He's got enough pressure on him now without worrying about a record," Steve said. "Just keep it quiet."

The heat was beginning to slow Bob a little. He didn't fan anyone in the eighth and finished off the ninth by getting Lary on strikes again. That was number fifteen, just one short of the Rube's record.

Bob wasn't aware of anything but that the Indians led 4 to 1 and he had pitched a complete game for his first big league triumph.

The reporters were waiting in the sweltering dressing room for Feller. The Indians crowded around Bob, congratulating him, and O'Neill came over to shake hands.

"Where's the guy who asked me a certain question before the game?" O'Neill asked loudly, sly innocence in his eyes. A reporter sheepishly waved his hand.

"Well," Steve asked, "does this answer your question?"

"Sure does," the writer agreed. "And a lot of others, too."

Across the field, another scribe cornered Hornsby.

"What do you think of that kid pitcher," he asked. "Kinda green, isn't he?"

"Green? Sure," answered Hornsby, one of the great hitters of all time and a man who always took his baseball seriously. "But he's only seventeen. With that fast ball, he could be as green as a Christmas tree. You're gonna hear a lot more about this kid."

In the Cleveland dressing room, Feller felt drawn and tired. Even a shower and brisk rub by Lefty didn't help. It had been an eventful day of high emotional strain. The reaction was setting in.

He and Weatherly were the last players out. Neither spoke as they walked slowly to the exit.

They went through the door into the street and suddenly they were surrounded by a horde of teenagers waving pads and pencils, clamoring for autographs.

Bob looked helplessly at Roy.

Roy answered with a grin. "Sign 'em," he commanded. "You're a hero now." Bob did.

"You may as well get used to it, kid," Weatherly said. He was only a few years older than Feller, but far more worldly.

A steak dinner and a movie show ended a perfect day. Then to bed, since the Indians entrained the next day on their most important eastern trip of the campaign.

CHAPTER FOURTEEN

Bob's next start was in Fenway Park against the Boston Red Sox, with the eastern trip already soured for the Indians by three losses in Washington.

The nearby left field wall, only 312 feet from the plate, gave Bob a closed-in feeling. Fenway Park is not a favorite with pitchers.

Feller pitched the second game of a Sunday double-header following a 3 to 2 defeat in the opener. Nothing went right for him. His control was off and he was in the hole against almost every batter.

Jimmy Foxx was Bob's personal nemesis that day, banging him for three hits and driving in three runs. Bob walked three and wild-pitched once, but the figures were more merciful than the facts. He was bad and he knew it.

O'Neill took him out of the game in the fifth inning, and the Bosox went on to a 5 to 1 victory. It was Feller's first defeat in the majors.

"You've got to expect these things," O'Neill explained to him later that evening. "You let Fenway Park get you. You were pressing."

"Maybe," Bob admitted, his spirits at low ebb, "but what

good is a pitcher if he can't turn it on when he has to?"

Steve shook his head wisely. "A great ballplayer can relax under pressure. When you press, you tighten your muscles. There's no power or speed in tight muscles. Remember that."

Bob's despair increased a week later in New York. Pitching against Lefty Gomez, Feller lasted only one inning in the worst performance of his life.

He started off by striking out Frank Crosetti, but then walked three Yankees and was banged for hits by Joe Di-Maggio, Tony Lazzeri, and Jackie Saltzgaver. To cap matters, he committed a balk.

In all, Bob yielded five runs and never got back in the game for the second inning. O'Neill mercifully removed him for a pinch hitter.

Bob was a sad and chastened young man after that experience. There was a lot more to pitching and winning in the big leagues than fogging in the fast one, he realized.

The trip home was blue for Bob and the Indians, whose flag hopes had taken a terrible beating in the east.

Like the answer to an unspoken prayer, Bill Feller was waiting for his son when the club arrived in Cleveland.

"Dad," Bob shouted on spotting his father. He hugged the older man unashamedly, surprised at the depth of his feelings.

"Figured it was time I came to see a ball game," Bill drawled shyly. He looked tired, Bob thought, and older. It was the first time they had been parted so long, giving each the chance to form new perspectives.

For his part, Bill saw a husky young man standing before him. Bob wore a neat summer suit, a colorful open-necked shirt, and natty sport shoes. He was bronzed, firmer around the jaw, and more assured. He's growing up, Bill thought proudly.

They had a great deal to discuss in the few days Bill stayed in Cleveland, most of it baseball directly concerned with Bob's pitching.

"You're just frightening yourself," his father said. "There's a lot you don't know about pitching, but you've got enough on the ball to get by."

They worked for hours on Bob's windup in the hotel room in front of the mirror. O'Neill and Schang had been cutting down Bob's motion and reducing the height of his kick with the left leg.

They talked about the family, the farm, and the neighbors. With Bill around, Bob resumed pitching with renewed confidence. Even Schang noticed it, telling O'Neill one afternoon: "The old man's visit is better than medicine."

Bob was told he would pitch in the Labor Day doubleheader against the Browns. By that time, the Indians were on the descent in the American League, tied with the Senators for fourth place.

Feller entered the game resolved to throw easier and to use the curve ball that O'Neill and Uhle had been teaching him. He stuck to it for exactly one batter, lead-off hitter Lyn Lary.

Lary popped up on Bob's soft stuff, but the Brownie bench immediately spotted the change and began riding the young pitcher.

"What happened to the old squirrel rifle?" one player shouted. A few more of the same jibes and Bob forgot his strategy. He began firing the ball on every pitch.

Bob wound up striking out ten and giving seven hits in the 7 to 1 victory. Tempering Bob's joy was the fact Jim Bottomley rapped him for four hits and Sam West for two. These were experienced batsmen who had adjusted to Feller's smoky hurling.

The Yankees came in next, clinching the pennant and stamping the Tribe down to fifth place. It was frustrating for O'Neill, helplessly aware how ruinous was his lack of pitching. It was a prime reason Steve could afford to go along with Feller as a starter.

O'Neill openly was criticized for risking Feller's mound future for what was construed as box-office avidity. Bob paid no heed to the newspapers. All he cared about was the chance to pitch regularly the rest of the season.

The next game for Bob was Sunday, September 13, against the Philadelphia Athletics. Connie Mack made it an unofficial Kids Day by starting Randy Gumpert, his eighteen-year-old star, against Feller.

Bob felt real strong. He faced a lineup of right-handed free swinging batters, theoretically perfect for a right-handed fast-ball hurler.

It was a weird game and a wonderful one. Bob was never faster—and seldom wilder. He had fearsome speed, and his curve was breaking a mile. But no one near the plate was safe.

The strikeouts mounted, inning after inning. So did the walks. By the sixth inning everyone in the park was aware the strikeout record was in danger. Bob had fanned twelve, with three innings to go.

Bob added two more in the seventh and another pair in the eighth, to tie the American League mark of sixteen. Who cared about the walks, the wild pitches, or even that he had hit Wally Moses in the ribs? Or that nine A's had stolen bases on his windup?

The crowd was rooting fiercely for Feller now. In the dugout, the Indians were pulling just as hard for the rookie pitcher.

"Keep bearing down, Bob," Trosky told him. Weatherly said nothing, merely pursing his lips and waving a clenched fist in silent support.

Bob felt the strain in the ninth inning. The fast ball lacked its former zip, but the curve was working nicely. The first two men up went out quickly, one on a pop-up and the other on a grounder to short.

Weariness settled on Bob like an invisible cloak. It was tough just winding up. He walked Charlie Moss, batting for Gumpert, and George Puccinelli came up.

The count went to three and two, as Puccinelli laid off the bad ones he had bitten for earlier in the game.

The Greek called time and walked out to the mound. "How do you feel?" he asked.

"Tired," Bob admitted. "But not dead."

"Think you can blow one past this bird?" There was doubt in the Greek's question.

"That's what he'll be expecting," Feller said. "He won't be looking for a curve."

"Okay," the catcher said. "Break it off good."

Bob cranked up with the full motion. He didn't care about stolen bases now. This was the pitch. He gripped the ball hard, spun and let go.

It darted inside, then hooked across the center of the plate, buckle high. Puccinelli stood blinking. The umpire's arm went up. "Strike three!"

The crowd jumped up, shouting and whooping. Some fans leaped the barriers and charged out to the exhausted pitcher, already surrounded and pounded by his own teammates.

It was a new league record, tying Dizzy Dean's seventeen strikeout mark for the majors. Bob, tired and overwhelmed by the ovation, had to be escorted back to the dugout.

Through the turmoil and the shouting, Bob spotted his father in his box seat. He hadn't moved, calmly sitting there all alone enjoying the fuss, the familiar tight little smile flicking at the corners of his mouth.

Bob lacked the strength to wave. But he knew how his father felt, deriving a strangely fierce satisfaction at being able to repay him in this fashion.

When the reporters clustered around, Bob learned more of the details of the game. He wasn't too happy about the nine walks or the nine stolen bases, but winning 5 to 2 and fanning seventeen was good enough.

That night at dinner, his dad seemed preoccupied and thoughtful.

"What's the matter, Dad," Bob asked, over the dessert. "Anything wrong with the game? Shucks, you're not gonna start holding out on me now, Dad."

"No, the game was fine," Bill said. "That curve makes you a real pitcher now."

"Something's bothering you," Bob persisted. "Don't you feel well? Or is it Mom or . . ." Bob stared in alarm.

"Nothing like that," his father reassured him, with a wan smile. "And nothing for you to worry about. Just that there's a fuss about your contract."

"My contract?" Bob exclaimed, puzzled.

"Judge Landis is looking into a complaint," Bill explained. "They claim there's something improper about the way you were signed."

The words sounded like doom to the young man.

CHAPTER FIFTEEN

Slapnicka shrugged when Bob asked him about it the next day.

"You just pitch, Bob," he said, "and let your father and me handle it." Slapnicka tried to sound reassuring, but his concern was apparent. It left Bob uneasy and strangely fearful of the future.

Bob made two more starts before the big story broke. He lasted six innings and lost 6 to 3 to the Detroit Tigers with only five strikeouts, but five days later in Chicago limited the White Sox to two runs while his teammates hammered out seventeen.

The phone rang early that night. It was one of the Cleveland reporters with the team.

"My office just queried me," the reporter said, "on a story that Judge Landis may declare you a free agent. What about it?"

"I can't say anything about it," Bob stammered. He felt miserable.

"Why not?" the caller persisted.

"I can't . . . I don't know enough about it . . ."

The reporter gave up. He hadn't expected much from the kid, anyway.

The phone rang all night, until Bob's roommate told him to order the switchboard to stop all calls. The next morning the papers went all out on the story.

It started with a complaint by Lee Keyser, owner of the Western League's Des Moines club, to Judge Kenesaw Mountain Landis, Commissioner of Baseball, at the manner in which Feller had been signed.

Keyser maintained that Feller was not the legal property of the Indians because he had been signed directly off the sandlots, in violation of a major-minor league agreement.

The facts, as Keyser presented them, unquestionably were true. Feller never played with the Fargo-Moorehead Northern League team to which he originally was signed. Neither did he play with New Orleans, to which he was sold. Instead, after injuring his arm, Bob had gone directly to the Indians.

The Cleveland club maintained it was sheer technicality, the very sort which had been going on in both leagues. Evidently the other owners, all of whom were anxious to sign Feller if he did become a free agent, agreed with the Indians. Not much later, at the annual baseball meeting, the club owners voided the sandlot agreement with the minors.

Still, under existing baseball law, the Feller case had to be disposed of, one way or the other. If it was an uncomfortable situation for Bob, who really had nothing to lose—as a free agent his signature was worth $100,000 to several other teams—it was dynamite for Judge Landis.

An adverse decision was sure to stir up a storm. The Cleveland club was certain to challenge it and probably gain the backing of both leagues, in which case the rugged-minded judge would have to reverse his decision or resign.

Besides, there probably were fifty other similar contracts throughout the majors which would be invalidated by such a ruling. Too many major league scouts had signed players directly off the sandlots or with cover-ups so scanty they never could stand up in court.

Before ruling, Judge Landis decided to speak to the Fellers. He summoned the youngster and his father for an interview in the Commissioner's Chicago office.

"Do I have to go?" Bob asked Slapnicka.

The general manager nodded glumly. Landis' decision was most important for him, too.

"Suppose I'm made a free agent?" Bob continued. "What then?"

"You'd be free to sign with any club," Slapnicka replied with a dejected shrug, "except Cleveland."

Despite the enormous amount of money it meant, Bob didn't want to become a free agent. He felt comfortable and happy with the Indians. Slapnicka and O'Neill were kindly men, sincerely concerned with his welfare and development as a pitcher. It might be different elsewhere, Bob feared, in the way of all youngsters facing the unknown.

The interview with Landis was as frightening as Bob had imagined it would be. Accompanied by his father, Bob faced the Judge with a scared-kid feeling.

Bob could not be blamed for quailing inwardly. The Judge, with his direct, fierce stare, his bristling eyebrows, and harsh judicial manner cowed far older and more experienced men than the seventeen-year-old boy before him now.

He questioned Bill Feller briskly and efficiently, but not

in an unkindly manner. "I want all the facts," he had told them in opening the interrogation, "and I intend to get them."

Now he turned to Bob.

"How do you feel about this?" the Judge asked. "Are you happy in Cleveland?"

"Yes, sir," Bob said, firmly and clearly. "Very much. Mr. Slapnicka and Mr. O'Neill treat me fine. They are very fair and very patient with me."

"Would you prefer to stay with the club?" the Judge asked.

"Yes, sir. Definitely. I don't think I'd feel the same anywhere else." The way he stood up and talked to Landis surprised even Bob. He felt a new confidence and strength surge through him. He looked the Judge squarely in those bright, piercing eyes.

Later, strolling down Michigan Boulevard, Bob was startled at the sudden chuckle from his father. He looked quizzically at the older man.

"I'm just thinking of the way you told him off," his dad smiled. "If you pitch that way . . ." They both burst out laughing.

"What do you think he'll do?" Bob asked, the worry returning.

His father was oddly cheerful. . . . "I think you'll stay where you are," he answered promptly. "What else can he do?"

What else indeed! The newspapers were full of conjecture. Opinion was evenly divided. Some wrote that Landis had to free Feller. Others pointed out that a million dollars in player material was at stake and that owners never would take the rap.

Meanwhile, the season was drawing to a close. Bob got one more chance to pitch, beating the Tigers in a game shortened to six innings by rain.

The Indians finished fifth, 22½ games behind the Yankees. Feller wound up with five wins and three losses in his first season, with seventy-six strikeouts in sixty-two innings. He gave up twenty-nine runs (twenty-three of them earned), fifty-two hits, and walked forty-seven.

The farewells were sad for Bob. His brief fling at big league life had been sweet and he hated to part with it, especially to return to school. Bob had another year of high school left.

"Take care of the arm," O'Neill told him on parting. "And for Pete's sake, stay off that tractor!"

"Keep the hay out of your hair," the players kidded. "And don't dip your fingers in the till!"

They were needling Bob about his election as president of the senior class at Van Meter High. The students had voted the honor almost immediately after his seventeen strikeout performance against the A's.

In a way, Bob was happy to return home. He had missed his folks. He never realized the strength of the family bond until that day earlier in the summer when he had found his dad waiting for him at the train after the disastrous eastern trip.

Van Meter gave young Feller a warm welcome. His first day back at school was a boy's dream . . . teachers and classmates clustered about him . . . the principal greeting him . . . the younger kids trailing like the hero-worshipers they were.

The town threw a gala homecoming celebration, including a presentation of the keys to the city by Mayor John Jung-

94

man, and a speech by the Governor of Iowa, Clyde Herring.

It was almost too much for a boy still a month away from his eighteenth birthday, but Bob handled himself with astonishing poise and aplomb. "He's a man now, Mom," Bill whispered to Mrs. Feller during the ceremonies.

Even kid sister Marguerite got up on the stand to tell the folks how proud she was of brother Bob. Grandpa Ed Foret said his piece, too. It was a wonderful day, fittingly capped by a baseball game.

Bob pitched two innings for each team, one of them his father's Farmers Union Club. The fans gasped at Bob's blinding fast ball. So did the batters, eleven of whom struck out in his total of four innings on the mound.

For the first time in his life, Bob buckled down seriously to his studies. He wanted his diploma. Five weeks behind the others, there were a lot of studies to catch up on. Besides, he'd be leaving earlier in the spring to go south with the ball club. Slapnicka arranged for a tutor during spring training.

Life at home was sweet. Bob never realized how much he could enjoy performing the simple chores around the farm. The crops were in, but there still was plenty of work to do. The myriad small joys of everyday routine were magnified for him now—his mother cheerfully bustling about the kitchen, his sister playing with her dolls, his dad walking out of the barn just before supper and asking him if he wanted to play catch.

Most of all, he secretly relished the respect his father commanded around town. The barbershop crowd and the neighboring farmers neither mocked nor doubted Bill Feller's sanity now. The baseball crop had paid off!

Then, on December 10, Judge Landis announced his decision.

Bob was in school when the news came and Bill Feller drove in immediately for him. The phone rang constantly and a horde of reporters headed for the farm for an interview.

On the ride home, Bob learned how Landis solved the dilemma. Feller remained Cleveland property, but the Indians had to pay Des Moines $7,500. It was a masterpiece of legal expediency.

The impending battle of the bank roll was dissolved. The emissaries of other big league clubs, waiting in Des Moines for the word which would have unleashed them on the Fellers with fantastic sums of money, folded their checkbooks and slunk home.

Guesses as to how much Feller might have commanded for his services ranged from $100,000 to $250,000. Bib Falk of the Red Sox admitted he was there with a blank check. "My only orders," he said, "are to get Feller."

That was academic now. Bob seemed more perturbed about the pittance Keyser got from the Indians than the enormous bonus he had been denied. "It's a joke," he exclaimed. "I never would have signed with Des Moines. I never even worked out with them."

He was happy to stay with Cleveland, Bob told reporters. "Looks like we'll have a good chance next year," he said. "I'm glad we got Earl Whitehill in that trade with Washington." He spoke like a big leaguer now, too.

"How about salary?" someone asked.

Bill's father cut in quickly. "Bob's asking for $20,000," he said.

96

"That's right," Bob added. "We think that's a fair sum. After all, I'm not asking for a bonus."

Bob hustled back to school the same day. After classes, he worked out with the basketball varsity. As a professional athlete he could not play in varsity games, but practicing with the squad kept him in condition. That night, he helped an alumni team beat the varsity in the annual game with the grads.

Autumn turned to winter. The ground froze and snow blanketed Iowa. Bob settled into a routine—studies, basketball, farm chores and plenty of hot stove baseball talk with his dad.

On January 10, 1937, Bob Feller signed with Cleveland for a $10,000 salary. It was the highest ever paid to a kid player.

Spring is beautiful in Iowa, but Bob didn't see it that year. He left for Hot Springs, Arkansas, late in February to attend a baseball school run by Wally Schang.

CHAPTER SIXTEEN

Spring training was a boy's dream come true for young Feller.

After a week at Hot Springs, soaking up sunshine and the diamond wisdom of Wally Schang, Bob joined the first contingent of Indians in New Orleans. The bayou city was a revelation to a country boy.

The strange accents, the exotic foods, the colorful mélange of peoples, the sights, and most of all, the French Quarter, which was like another world to Bob, fascinated the young man. He spent hours exploring the city.

There wasn't too much time for sightseeing. Baseball occupied most of Bob's day. Then there were his high school studies with a tutor provided by the club. Boning up on math and history after exhausting hours on the diamond left little inclination for diversion.

As always, Feller threw himself zealously into spring baseball preparations. Too zealously, thought O'Neill.

"Take it slowly," Steve warned, "I don't even want you to throw the first week. Just get in shape."

At his age and with his rugged farm background, Bob reveled in the training program. Most of the others, including the younger players, griped and groaned. Bob was ready and eager to cut loose with all his steam, right from the start.

Wisely, O'Neill and Schang rode herd on him constantly. They worked on his curve and added a changeup pitch. Bob wasn't confident about the letup, but the curve pleased him enormously. It snapped off real big now.

By the end of March, the Indians were ready to begin their annual spring series with the New York Giants, the pennant winners in the National League, who had lost to the New York Yankees in six games in the 1936 World Series.

Bob was as curious about the Giants as they were about him. Left-handed pitcher Carl Hubbell and home run slugger Mel Ott were the stars of the New York team managed by Bill Terry. They were anxious to see how fast this young strikeout sensation could throw.

They found out in the first game of the exhibition series in Vicksburg. Bob worked three innings against the Giants and held them hitless, striking out six batters, four in a row. Hubbell and Ott were frank in their admiration, as were their teammates. All, that is, but one.

"He's not so fast," insisted Dick Bartell, the fiery shortstop. "There's two or three guys faster in our league."

"Name one," someone asked in the Giant dugout and the others snickered as Bartell's face reddened. Dick's temper didn't improve when he popped out to the infield and Feller continued to fan batter after batter.

"Van Mungo's faster," Bartell usually would say, and his fellow Giants would razz him. It became a dugout routine when Feller pitched.

Naturally, word of Rowdy Dick's low opinion of him got back to Bob. He said nothing. Feller didn't know or care whether he threw faster than anyone else, but it did hurt that Bartell would go out of his way to knock him.

That spring Feller faced Bartell nineteen times. Not only did Dick fail to get a hit, he struck out sixteen times! After each humiliation, Bartell stubbornly would insist, "He's not so fast. He won't last." It always drew a laugh among the Giants.

That Feller was a box office magnet was evident in the way people flocked to see him against the Giants. There were 11,000 in the stands at New Orleans when he opposed Hubbell. Bob went five innings, held the league champs hitless again, and struck out six.

Bob had a sickening scare in this game. Hank Leiber, the burly outfield slugger, tried to duck away from a high inside curve that didn't break properly and was struck a glancing blow on the head. He went down and the crowd suddenly was deathly quiet.

Bob, aghast, stood paralyzed for a moment before breaking for the plate. Fortunately, the ball hit Leiber's shoulder first, enough to slow it down somewhat, and he was all right. X rays showed neither fracture nor concussion.

For Bob, it was a close call. He wasn't a brush-off pitcher, and never did become one. His great speed and reputation for occasional wildness kept batters wary. Shaken, he served up a fat pitch to the next Giant, who lambasted it out of the park—foul, luckily. Feller settled down after that.

The exhibition trip north was tiring and boring. Both teams lived out of suitcases in their Pullman specials, touring through Texas, Oklahoma, Arkansas, Alabama, Georgia, South Carolina, and North Carolina before winding up at the Polo Grounds.

Bob opposed Hubbell again in the finale, attracting 31,000 to the Harlem ballpark. Both pitched eight innings, with the Indians ahead 4 to 2 when Bob departed. It concluded twenty-seven innings against the Giants for Feller in which he had struck out thirty-seven hitters, allowed only seven runs, and had not lost a game.

Back in Cleveland, Feller was the sensation of the spring. One paper was publishing his life story, and hordes of magazine writers were preparing feature articles about him.

The Indians with Mel Harder pitching, opened in Detroit, losing, 4 to 3 to the Tigers. Bob didn't learn that he would pitch against the Browns the day after the team's return to Cleveland until just before warmup time. He sucked in his breath, tightened his belt, and strode out to the mound.

The first man up was Billy Knickerbocker, traded by the Indians in a winter deal with St. Louis. Feller had a one-and-one count when he decided to throw a fast curve. He wound up and let the ball go, ending up with a violent snap of the wrist.

A sharp, searing pain raced up his forearm into the elbow. Bob stumbled off the mound clutching his arm. It hurt terribly, but Feller tried to conceal it. He didn't want anyone to think he was a quitter.

Frankie Pytlak, the catcher, kept calling for the curve, and Bob kept shaking him off. It was all he could do to throw a fast ball. The inning was disastrous. Bob allowed four runs on two hits and four walks.

He said nothing to O'Neill between innings. The arm still hurt, although the pain had diminished to a steady, hot throb. With one out in the second, his mind concentrated on his arm more than on the batter, Bob walked three men to fill the bases.

Up stepped Rogers Hornsby, player-manager of the Browns. He had poled a 450-foot homer against Johnny Allen the day before. Bob struck him out. There still was lightning left in his fast ball.

He fanned Clift to end the inning, then got the next three men up in the third frame. By the sixth inning, Feller had struck out eleven Brownies. The arm felt better until he tried another curve. The same stabbing sensation shot through his arm again. It was time to speak up.

Even-tempered O'Neill came close to shouting in anger when Bob told him about the arm. He shook his head in dismay.

"That was foolish," he told Bob. "I hope you haven't caused serious damage to your arm."

Feller went directly to the locker room with Lefty Weisman, who applied hot towels and salving chatter to calm Feller's fears.

Slapnicka and O'Neill were in to see Feller after the game.

"It could be a stretched ligament," Lefty suggested. Slapnicka and Steve said nothing, merely looking glum.

"We'll have Doc Castle look at it tomorrow," Slapnicka said.

X rays the next day showed nothing. Dr. Ed Castle, the team physician, could find nothing. Lefty continued his rubs, heat treatment, and anything else that came to mind. The arm still pained.

The reporters made it a front-page story. Some jumped Slapnicka and O'Neill for rushing the kid pitcher, accusing them of sacrificing a promising career for immediate gate profits. Others called Bob a flash in the pan. A few predicted Feller would be back as good as ever.

Through it all, Bob lived in despair and fear. Sitting around as everyone else played was taking its emotional toll. Slapnicka observed Feller's mounting depression with concern.

"How would you like to go home for a spell?" he asked one day. "You have to get back for graduation anyway. You may as well go a bit earlier."

It was a welcome change for Bob. The Indians were playing well, the batters hitting, and the pitchers working on a four-man rotation with Allen, Harder, Galehouse, and Whitehill.

Bob flew home, landing at Des Moines. He was stunned at the reception. Hundreds of friends and fans from Van Meter and nearby communities were waiting at the airport to greet him. His parents, Mother beaming and Dad proud but anxious, were there.

Bob wasn't allowed to forget the arm. It was always the same question, no matter whom he met. Politely and patiently, Bob answered as best he could. Meanwhile, he attended school, took his final exams, passed, and was graduated.

Slapnicka sent him to several other doctors on his return to Cleveland, to no avail. Feller's arm hurt when he threw a curve. He was desperate and so was Slapnicka. It was June and the Indians had begun to slip. The pitching had fallen apart and the team was in fifth. The papers were openly critical of his handling of Feller.

Slapnicka heard of a local chiropractor, named A. L. Austin, located close by League Park. "Let's try him," he told O'Neill. "We've tried everyone else."

Doc Austin was licensed to manipulate bone and muscle. A stocky man with powerful hands, neither Doc Austin nor his shabby office was impressive. Another wasted journey, Bob thought.

Bob's pessimistic appraisal must have showed on his face. The stubby little therapist, a smile in his eyes, gently took Feller's arm.

"We get a lot of ballplayers you never hear about," he said, "and fix 'em up real good."

"Can you fix me?" Bob asked, naively.

"That depends," Austin answered, as his fingers probed Bob's arm. "If it's what I think it is . . ." He lapsed into silence as he continued his examination.

Finally he looked up at Slapnicka. "It's the ulna bone," Austin said. "It's out of the socket."

He took hold of Bob's wrist with one hand and the elbow with another.

"This'll hurt for a second," he warned. Then he tugged, suddenly and powerfully.

A wild flash of pain shot through Bob like a jolt of electricity, racing from the elbow to every nerve in his body. Blinding lights exploded in his head. He felt dizzy for a moment. Then suddenly the pain was gone. Bob felt limp.

"That's it," Austin said. "Rest it for a day and then, well, you can throw as hard as you like."

Slapnicka, his eyes round with worry and his cheeks pale as alabaster, nodded to Bob.

"You mean I can throw anything?" Bob asked, uncertainly.

"Anything you could throw before," Austin said laconically. "That arm will never bother you again. I get a lot of golfers and ballplayers with the same thing. Never had a recurrence."

Walking back, both Feller and the Cleveland vice-president were steeped in thought. Bob wondered if the Doc was a fake. Slapnicka wondered whether he had done the right thing. If Feller's arm wasn't cured . . . he dreaded the thought.

The next twenty-four hours dragged slowly for Bob. He couldn't wait to try out the arm. All evening, he prodded and twisted it without feeling a twinge of pain. The next day, he reported at the ball park, hurried into his baseball togs, and rushed out to the field.

O'Neill and Slapnicka were waiting. Steve had a mitt on his hand. "I'll catch you, myself," he said.

Bob warmed up easily. The arm felt fine. He turned on a bit more speed. It still felt good.

"I'm gonna open up now," he said after a while. All three were tense as Bob wound up, reared back and threw. The ball whistled in and landed in O'Neill's mitt with a loud report.

Bob threw several more as hard as he could. No pain.

Bob's arm went back, his foot up, and then he threw. The ball shot in, dipped, and hooked.

"Beautiful." Steve jumped into the air. Then he remembered. "How does it feel?"

Bob's wide grin was sufficient answer. "Great," he shouted. "Just great."

Steve let out a whoop, and the more dignified Slapnicka resisted a desire to do the same. Instead, he compromised on a long sigh of relief and a silent prayer of thanks.

CHAPTER SEVENTEEN

The elbow never bothered Feller again. His first test against the Tigers on July 4 was highly successful, for the arm if not exactly for Bob.

O'Neill kept him in the game only four innings. Bob was strong and fast, but he was wild, too. He struck out three in a row, including Charlie Gehringer and Hank Greenberg, in the second inning. But a walk, a wild throw, an error, and Detroit's lone hit added up to three runs in the fourth, enough to chalk him with the defeat.

A week later, he tackled the same team again, this time in Detroit, and gave only two hits in 8⅔ innings. But he lost again, 3 to 2, on six walks and a wild throw that let in the winning run.

It was Bob's third straight loss and he was disconsolate. This new outbreak of wildness on the mound worried him. "It's the change of pace," Bob told Schang. "I'm going to drop it for a while. It's throwing me off."

A week went by as the big youngster fretted and fumed in his eagerness to pitch. The murderous Yankees came in and O'Neill named Feller to hurl on Sunday. Close to 60,000 spectators were in the Cleveland park when Bob walked to the hill.

The Yankees were loaded with power. Gehrig was having a smashing season. Joe DiMaggio was belting homers faster and further than anyone in the majors. The New York team had great fielding and great pitching.

Equally important to Bob, the family—Mom, Pop, and Sis—was in the jam packed stands to watch him pitch.

Feller was fast but wild. He fanned a lot of Yankees, but he walked a lot too. DiMag hit a freak double, which scored a run in the third. Sammy Hale bobbled Joe's drive at third and Red Rolfe, tearing past, accidentally kicked it out of reach.

Now it was the ninth inning, the score tied at 1 to 1. Red Ruffing, the opposing hurler and fine batman, led off with a sharp single. Feller messed up on the play on Frank Crosetti's sacrifice by hitting the runner on the throw to first. Still angry at himself, he walked Rolfe to fill the bags.

Joe DiMaggio, who had walloped a triple in his previous time up, strode to the plate. The crowd was tense and expectant. Bill Feller dug his fingers into the seats, staring grimly at the boy on the mound. His wife, stealing a glance at the giant farmer, bit her lip nervously. Only eight-year-old Marguerite seemed unconcerned and happy.

DiMag didn't move a muscle as Feller blew two fast balls by for strikes. With his matchless eyes, the Yankee Clipper could afford to wait for the pitch he wanted.

The next one was it.

Pytlak signaled for a curve. Bob looked at the runners, wound up, and threw. DiMag's bat whipped around, caught the ball on the nose just as Joe's big shoulders got behind it. Bob knew as soon as he heard the crack.

The white pellet streaked out high and fast . . . rising . . . rising . . . to plummet into the stands in left center. A grand slam homer, DiMag's twenty-fourth circuit of the season.

Plodding off the field, his head down, after the 5 to 1 defeat, Bob was startled by a firm grip on his shoulder. He turned. It was the Yankee first baseman, Lou Gehrig, a smile on his strong face.

"Don't let it get you, kid," he said. "You've got plenty on the ball." Lou grinned and walked away. These gracious words from one of the greats of baseball lifted Bob's sagging spirits.

No one said anything in the locker room except the usual perfunctory consolations. The team was morose. Bob felt he had let the club down.

"What did you throw DiMaggio?" his father asked, later that evening after dinner. Bob told him it was a curve.

"Don't you know the way he stands he murders a curve?" Bill asked. Bob nodded glumly.

"Then why did you throw it?"

"My catcher called for it," Bob replied.

"Don't you know how to move your head from side to side—like this?" the older man continued, making the universal sign that means no in any language.

"Yes, sir," Bob answered humbly.

It was the fourth defeat for Bob, who finally won four days later in a one-inning relief stint against the Athletics. He added another, 11 to 2, over the route against the Senators in Washington, striking out nine and walking three, before tangling with the Yankees again.

The Indians had gone bad again, with mounting criticism from the press and cruel pressure on O'Neill, who suffered unjustly for the fielding lapses and spotty hitting of his team. Young as he was, Bob could understand what the manager was going through.

Feller had a strange day against the Bronx Bombers. He struck out twelve, but allowed ten hits and ten walks. Gehrig's homer with two on in the ninth tied the score at 5 to 5. Bob was taken out in the tenth inning when Myril Hoag singled.

The Yankees won 7 to 6. Although the defeat was not charged to Feller, he felt responsible. That pitch to Gehrig . . . Bob burned with chagrin.

The tribe returned to Cleveland in bad shape mentally. They had dropped eleven of thirteen games on the road and sunk to fifth place in the American League standing.

The tide turned during that home stand, for Feller and his teammates. Bob picked up his third win, beating the Browns in a six-strikeout job. He went eight innings to no decision against the Chicago White Sox, leaving for a pinch hitter in a game eventually lost.

It wasn't until August that Bob hit his first real winning stride. Facing the Boston Red Sox, he fanned sixteen, walked four and gave as many hits. His control pleased Bob most, but he wasn't happy about the Red Sox player who stole home on him in the 8 to 1 victory.

Then came a disappointing performance against the Senators, who chased Feller in the seventh for his fifth loss. Perhaps Bob had something else on his mind—the coming invasion by the Yankees and a chance to get back at the proud champions.

Schang, who roomed with Feller, was surprised to see Bob get into bed at eight o'clock the night before the game with the Yankees.

"Are you sick?" Wally asked.

"Nope," Bob replied, "I'm making sure to be rested for tomorrow. I'm just gonna pour it on full speed as far as I can go."

Bob did just that, beating the Bombers 4 to 2.

DiMag, imperturbable as ever, spoiled a shutout with his homer in the eighth. Bob added twelve more strikeouts to his burgeoning total of ninety-nine in 104 innings. He was particularly happy about fanning Lou Gehrig three straight times.

The Indians were as torrid as the weather in September, winning twenty-four of thirty-eight games. Feller contributed five, second only to Allen's seven wins in that month.

The only worm in the apple was another defeat by the Yankees in New York. After leading 4 to 0 for seven innings, Feller succumbed to wildness. He walked three men and gave two hits to tie the score, before leaving the game. The Indians ultimately won, but Harder got the credit.

Bob's last appearance of the 1937 season was a 4 to 1 win over the White Sox in Chicago. It gave Feller a 9 to 7 record in a total of twenty-six games and 149 innings pitched. He had fanned 150, walked 100, and showed an earned run average of 3.38.

All in all, it was a splendid record for a youngster in his first full season of major league baseball. Bob's ERA mark was ninth in the league and his strikeout average topped all others, although Lefty Gomez of the Yankees struck out more, 194 batters in 278 innings.

The time for farewells was sad for Bob. He had heard enough locker room gossip to realize this probably was good-by to O'Neill as Cleveland manager. He would miss this gentle, capable ex-catcher.

O'Neill knew it too when he shook hands with Feller.

"So long, Bob," Steve said, with what Bob interpreted as a slightly wistful expression. "You're going to be a great pitcher. Remember that. Maybe even by next year . . ." He slapped Bob's shoulder and that was it.

Bob spent a few days at home before leaving on a barnstorming tour with a group of major leaguers rounded up by Ray Doan. It was, Bob thought, an easy and pleasant way of picking up a sizable chunk of money.

Bob was just coming off the diamond in a small town in the southwest when he heard the news. It was October 20.

"Hey, Bob," someone shouted. "You got a new boss. O'Neill's out. Vitt's got the job."

Oscar Vitt, Feller thought. He had heard about him. A driving, forceful man who had managed the Newark Bears, a Yankee organization club, to the International League pennant that year.

Bob shrugged. He didn't qualify as an expert, but he couldn't see how anyone could improve on O'Neill. Time would tell, he figured.

CHAPTER EIGHTEEN

That winter was one of the happiest of Bob's life. He
signed a new contract for 1938 at $20,000 and celebrated by
taking the family to Florida.

For the first time, Bob felt he was repaying his folks for
what they had done for him. He had never seen his father
enjoy himself as much or be as carefree.

Time passed too quickly. It was almost like a dream. From
Florida to Iowa to New Orleans. Life was moving rapidly
and fabulously for a boy just turned nineteen.

Training camp was a different proposition under Vitt.
There were many new faces in the Cleveland retinue. Wally
Schang stayed on as a coach, while Johnny Bassler, another
former catcher, was added. The energetic Vitt was all over
the place.

"We'll have to make some changes in your style," he told
Bob briskly one day. They were sitting around with Schang
and Bassler. "The base runners will steal the shirt right off
your back if you don't change," he said.

"Your windup is too long and too slow," Vitt rattled on.
Bob watched him with fascination. Vitt did everything with
dash and purpose. He spoke, thought, and even walked

quickly. His prodigious energy had an almost exhausting effect on others.

"You've had enough time with the club to adjust to changes," Vitt decided. "Don't kick so high and don't bring the leg up so slowly on the windup."

Feller wasn't the only Cleveland player to feel the force of Vitt's driving personality. In one way or another, every member of the team was influenced. Some resented Vitt's insistence on hustle, his constant corrections, and his strict new club regulations, but most of the Indians accepted him. He would tone down after a while, they felt.

The change-over in pitching style was difficult for Bob, but he worked at it conscientiously. The shorter kick and faster motion disturbed his throwing rhythm, cutting down his speed but increasing his control.

The Giants noticed it immediately when the two old spring exhibition rivals resumed their annual series. "He's not as fast," they said, after Feller worked three innings against them and struck out only two batters.

Bob didn't mind. For one thing, he didn't walk anyone and gave only two hits.

Then, more important, his arm felt wonderful. "Let 'em talk," he told Schang. "I'm not taking any chances. I learned my lesson last year."

This was not the same wide-eyed country boy who had come to camp a year ago. A season in the majors, traveling to the big cities, living in the company of sophisticated ballplayers, meeting people in all stations of life, Bob already was mature beyond his nineteen years.

His long, placid face, his farm background and ways, and his natural reticence with strangers created a deceptively different impression. Bob didn't say much, but he knew what he wanted.

Bob's teammates knew him as a quiet, sober youngster not given to the wild life. He wasn't much for card playing or any form of gambling and he didn't intrude on others, but he came up with surprisingly clever and apt observations in conversation and had a sharp sense of humor.

He saw and absorbed everything through shrewd eyes which missed nothing and registered everything on a mind which never forgot.

If the Indians as a group were not warmly enthusiastic about Feller as a personality or companion, they definitely respected him both as an individual and a ballplayer. Bob got along well with everyone on the squad.

He wasn't excited when Vitt informed him he would pitch the second game of the season against the Browns, who had beaten Johnny Allen in the opener. He wasn't excited in the game, either, as he mowed the St. Louis batters down with regularity.

All Bob thought of as he worked was that his fast ball still didn't seem as good as last year. He wasn't pouring the ball past the hitters nor getting many strikeouts, but by the sixth inning, the sparse crowd and both dugouts were aware that Feller hadn't given a hit.

Only Bob didn't seem to realize it. When Billy Sullivan, who had been traded by Cleveland to the Browns, bunted to Feller's right and beat out the throw to first, the pitcher was about the only member of the Tribe who didn't dispute the decision with the umpire.

It turned out to be the only hit of a 9 to 0 shut-out win. There didn't seem to be much drama after Sullivan's hit, but

Bob was a highly satisfied young man despite six walks and only six strikeouts. He had gotten two hits, scoring one run and driving in two others.

"Some hitting, eh?" he said, joshing Rollie Hemsley, his catcher.

"Some catching, you mean," Rollie grinned back.

Of all the players, Bob felt most comfortable with Hemsley, easily the wildest and most uninhibited of the Indians. Vitt had acquired him from the Browns that spring, despite a reputation for fun which had earned him the sobriquet of Rollickin' Rollie.

But playful as he was off the field, Hemsley was a bear for work on the field. To Bob, he was the greatest catcher in the game. He had full confidence in Rollie's knowledge and utter admiration for his superb catching ability. There were few wild pitches with Hemsley behind the plate.

It was a fine start for what appeared to be a bright 1938 season for Bob, who swept to six victories, including a nine-strikeout, 3 to 2 conquest of the mighty Yankees, before the dark clouds began to gather for Bob and the Indians.

A cold in his back had been hindering Bob for a few weeks when Vitt sent him in for Johnny Allen in the sixth inning of the nightcap of a double-header in New York. A homer by Joe Gordon with one on, promptly put the Yanks ahead 7 to 6 for the ball game, narrowing the Cleveland lead over the Bronx Bombers to 1½ games.

Vitt pulled his forces together in a strong home stand capped by a twin-bill killing of the Yankees after Bob had beaten them 10 to 5. Hemsley talked to Bob after the game.

"You're not pitching right," he told Bob. "You're pointing. You're aiming the ball."

Mournfully, Bob could only agree. He knew Rollie was right, but he didn't know how to cut loose. He was so anxious to keep the runners close to base and not to walk anyone that he wasn't throwing easily. The rhythm and the power weren't there.

Feller proved his catcher's point by walking eight and losing 7 to 6 to the Tigers in the first game of a July 4 doubleheader. When the Indians dropped the nightcap behind Mel Harder, they no longer had the lead to themselves. The Yankees, winning in New York, now shared it with them.

The three-day break for the All-Star game at Cincinnati ruined the Indians. Allen, picked for the American League team along with Averill and Feller, slipped on a bar of soap in his hotel shower and banged his elbow. It hurt, but not enough to prevent him from pitching the next day. He was never the same the rest of the campaign.

The Tribe went downhill from that point. They lost close games, usually in such aggravating fashion that Vitt finally exploded with a tongue-lashing of the team which somehow managed to get into the newspapers and was the real beginning of the outspoken manager's later woes with the team.

Bob was in a depression. He could get the ball over, but not past the batters. He was afraid to go to the mound. The Red Sox blasted him in Boston, driving him off the mound with four runs in the third inning.

The papers were riding the Indians, Vitt, and Feller, too. Washed-up wonder boy, fading skyrocket, and premature flash were only a few of the things that went into print about the boy from Iowa.

When the Indians arrived home, Bob's family was waiting

for him in Cleveland. His father didn't have to ask Bob what was wrong.

"It's all up here," the farmer said, tapping his head with a bony finger. "You're letting the brain stop your arm from doing what it should."

Bob sighed, almost in pleasure despite the harsh truths he was hearing. It was wonderful just being with Dad again. Wonderful and reassuring, because Dad always put his finger on the trouble.

"Remember what I've always told you," his father continued. "It doesn't make any difference who's batting. You've got the arm. But don't forget to use your head, when you're pitching to all those big stars. Don't forget the arm and the head."

Bob won his next start 4 to 2, against the A's, after a shaky beginning, and the picture brightened temporarily. Bob was in and out, good and bad. As for the team, it was just bad. By August, they trailed the Yankees by fourteen games and relations between the players and Vitt were strained and tense.

The low point, absolute bottom, came for Bob in Yankee Stadium. It was the day after a big blow off in which the Indians disintegrated temperamentally right on the field. They fought with the umpires, with themselves, and with Manager Vitt. Several were ejected from the game and heavily fined.

Bob, surrounded by unpleasantness and tension, was miserable. Coming out of the dugout to face the Yankees, he never felt so unsure of himself. The Yankees completed the job.

They smashed and walloped him for fifteen hits. Gehrig and DiMaggio hammered homers, the latter driving in seven runs. Bob walked nine men. It was a nightmare.

Having experienced the worst, Bob suddenly relaxed. He lost his fear of the batter. He felt more comfortable with his new pitching style. His confidence was returning.

The first sign of his return to form as a fireballer was a 6 to o whitewashing of the Tigers in Detroit, where the great Hank Greenberg was blasting the fences in pursuit of Babe Ruth's record, sixty home runs. Bob beat the Tigers later in September, again holding Hank hitless with the big slugger's circuit total at fifty-six.

Greenberg had fifty-eight homers, with two games to play in Cleveland, on the final day of the season. Feller had just as great an incentive in his own eyes—his eighteenth victory of the season, which would make him the Indians' leading pitcher for the year.

Frank Pytlak was behind the bat for the Tribe and Bob never felt looser or faster. The ball threw off sparks on its way in and his curve broke like a ricocheting bullet.

The Tigers couldn't touch him. By the end of the fourth inning, Bob had ten strikeouts. He picked up two more in the fifth. Detroit broke the ice in the sixth with two runs on Cullenbine's single and doubles by Greenberg and Tebbetts, but Feller added two more strikeouts for a total of fourteen.

The crowd now was rooting for Feller to break Dizzy Dean's big league record more than they were pulling for Greenberg to beat the Bambino's homer mark. The big youngster fanned Harry Eisenstat, the opposing pitcher, for No. 15 in the seventh.

Bob was tired now. He was losing control of his fast ball, which meant he had to slow it down to get it across the plate.

The eighth was a rough inning. He walked Cullenbine and

Greenberg, Tebbetts sacrificed, and Chet Laabs whiffed for the fourth time. A walk and Christman's single, scoring two more runs, came before Feller retired the side.

In the ninth, he fanned Foxx on three power pitches for his No. 17. He needed just one more strikeout for the record. Cullenbine singled, and Greenberg flied out his pursuit of Babe Ruth's record destroyed. Tebbetts drew a walk.

Now it was Laabs at the plate again. A rookie outfielder with a weakness for a high fast pitch, hapless Chet had fanned four times. His eyes were narrowed in worry and determination, his lips a tight line as he swung his bat.

Bob pushed all compassion out of his heart. This was the big leagues, where you had to sink or swim. For him it meant getting that eighteenth strikeout. For Laabs, it meant averting humiliation by getting a hit. Neither would be giving anything away.

Bob fired. It was a strike. The next pitch was low for a ball. Bob broke a curve over the plate for strike two.

Bob looked at Pytlak for the signal. He shrugged it off. He felt Laabs would be looking for the hook. He wound up, then threw. The ball streaked across the inside corner. Strike three!

It was over and the Indians swarmed around Bob, pounding his back, tugging him, hauling, shoving, and shouting joyously as if they had won the pennant. It was a new strikeout record.

So ended the 1938 campaign for Bob Feller.

He had fanned 240, leading both leagues, and posted a 17 to 11 record. Only Red Ruffing, Bobo Newsom, and Lefty Gomez had won more games in the American League, while teammate Mel Harder had a slight statistical edge at 17 to 10.

While the figures suggested success, Bob went home far from proud or satisfied. He should have done better, he could do better, this resolute nineteen-year-old told himself as the train sped him closer to Van Meter, Iowa.

CHAPTER NINETEEN

Bob reported for spring training in 1939 as a veteran, no longer the shy lad who had to prove himself.

At New Orleans, the Indians greeted him like a brother, joking about his added weight and the fact he now shaved regularly. Bob trained cautiously, working more on his legs and wind than his pitching arm.

It was a poor spring for Feller and the Cleveland club. Dissension between the players and Vitt, resulting in a series of holdouts and flare-ups, slowed down the team. Although Bob tried to steer clear, he could not help being affected by the unpleasant atmosphere surrounding him.

Everything went wrong. The Indians lost all through the spring tour. Feller did little pitching and in several appearances was severely shellacked. Mel Harder's arm hurt. Johnny Allen wasn't in shape. Earl Averill held out so long, owner Alva Bradley called him a quitter. Jeff Heath was vigorously feuding with Vitt. Frank Pytlak left the club in a huff, but finally was wheedled back. Rollie Hemsley was in and out of the doghouse.

Still, Bob won the opener against Detroit with a three-hitter in which he walked only two men. The newspapers immediately noted the new firmness and maturity of his pitching, an embarrassing appraisal in view of his next showing against the Yankees, who drew ten walks and clobbered him for as many hits.

He had six wins to his credit before the Tribe headed east. He barely missed a no-hitter in Boston when Bobby Doerr slapped him for a single and repeated the feat against the Tigers in his first game under lights. Oddly, it was Averill, traded to Detroit only shortly before, who spoiled it for Bob with a single in the sixth inning.

This was Feller's twelfth win, an eighteen strikeout job, which clinched a berth in the All-Star game at the Yankee Stadium. Blasé as he may have seemed, playing in the All-Star game was a tremendous thrill for Bob. In fact, he was just as awed by the big names of baseball surrounding him as any hero-worshiping kid.

"How would you like to pitch today?" Hemsley, the only other Cleveland player on the All-Star squad, asked Bob as they warmed up in the sun. "Wouldn't be scared, would you?" Rollie grinned.

Bob grinned back at his fun-loving catcher.

"Who's afraid of that league!" he answered defiantly.

Bob watched in the bullpen for five innings before his chance came. Tommy Bridges, a canny Detroit pitcher, was leading the National Leaguers 3 to 1 when suddenly he was in trouble in the sixth.

The call was flashed to the bullpen for Feller to warm up. He didn't have much time to loosen his arm when Joe McCarthy, the great Yankee pilot, waved Feller into the game.

One out and the bases loaded, with Arky Vaughan, the solid slugger of the Pirates, at bat.

There were 63,000 fans in the stadium as Feller, chest out and head high, walked to the mound with the peculiar gait so many people mistook for a strut. "Looks cool as a cucumber, doesn't he?" marveled McCarthy.

Although he appeared calm, Bob was nervous, as he had a right to be in this situation. Vaughan was a vicious clutch hitter, with a keen eye and fast bat action. Bob studied the man at the plate, wound up, and let it ride.

It was a fast ball, low, and on the inside corner. Vaughan swung and topped a grounder to second. Joe Gordon gobbled it up, flipped to Joe Cronin, who shot it to Hank Greenberg at first for the double play. Feller was out of the inning on one pitch!

The crowd roared its appreciation of Feller's clutch skill and courage. They added to it as Bob mowed down the batters in the next three innings. He had everything—blinding speed, control, and a big curve.

The Nationals got to him for only one hit in the ninth, but Bob fanned Johnny Mize of the Cardinals and Stan Hack of the Cubs in the final frame to insure the 3 to 1 triumph.

Officially, Bridges was credited with the win, but to the baseball world this was Feller's victory.

National League players, officials, and reporters were clearly impressed. Even the Giants, who knew Bob from their annual spring series, noted the difference in his work. His motion was smooth, he didn't depend on speed alone, and he pitched with poise.

"Imagine him getting me on a changeup," laughed Mel Ott

of the Giants, later. Bob had fooled Mel on a three-and-one pitch, a daring delivery to Ott. It was the measure of Feller's development as a pitcher.

But while Feller moved from success to success during the campaign, the Indians floundered along in an aura of bickering and dissent. Vitt's fierce drive, his outspoken criticisms, his constant wrangling with players, and the consequent bitterness, established a destructive, hostile mood.

There were constant rumors of firings, trades, and upheavals. Once it was Vitt on his way out, then one or another of the dissident players. With curious reporters constantly sniffing about for a story, the issue never was allowed to die. It was a tragic case of mutual dislike and distrust between Vitt and his players.

It was at this critical point in the feud, with mounting rumors of a club-house rebellion brewing, that the Tribe faced the Yankees before 76,000 fans in a double-header at the Stadium in August.

Vitt was grim and pale, deep worry creases on his face as he told Bob he would pitch the first game. There was an unspoken question in Vitt's unhappy eyes and Feller felt a pang of pity for this furious fighter who had gotten off on the wrong foot with the team.

The Indians won both games, Feller gaining his sixteenth victory despite a rush of homer pitches. Harder took the nightcap with a superb four-hitter. Beating the hated Bombers twice was like soothing balm on irritated nerves.

On the return to Cleveland, the team was bolstered by the acquisition of the new, young keystone combination of Lou Boudreau at short and Ray Mack at second from the Buffalo Club of the International League.

These fast, skillful youngsters gave the Indians an enormous lift through the stretch, enough to push them from fourth to third in the standings on thirty-six wins in their last fifty-six games.

Bob wound up with twenty-four wins against nine losses, a golden year for a young man not yet of voting age. He led the league in total victories, struck out 246 in 297 innings, issued 142 walks, and was fifth in earned run averages with 2.85.

The experts agreed that Feller unquestionably had arrived. They said that if anyone was to win thirty games in one season in the near future, it would be the boy from Van Meter.

Someone pointed out that Bob's strikeout average had dropped from the previous year, and Feller came up with a prompt reply. "Strikeout and earned run averages are all right," he said, "but nothing counts like a win."

Before leaving for home, Bob agreed to terms with Slapnicka for 1940. They settled on $40,000 a year. "Pretty good pay for a hayseed," Bob kidded himself.

Back home, Bob bought himself a new car and went over plans to build his folks a brand-new brick house on the farm. He replenished his wardrobe in big city style.

Bob's cup of joy overflowed with the news that he had finished third behind Joe DiMaggio and Jimmy Foxx in the Most Valuable Player award balloting.

Proudest of all was his father, thinner and obviously not as healthy as he should be.

"Think you can win the pennant?" he asked Bob, one day that winter.

"We've got the club to do it," Bob answered. "Boudreau and Mack are a big help up the middle. We've got hitting and pitching."

"Sure," his father agreed. "But how about Vitt . . . ?"

Bob shrugged. There was no use talking about it.

CHAPTER TWENTY

The Indians trained at Fort Myers on the west coast of Florida in 1940. The weather was excellent, manager Vitt and the players seemed to be getting along, and word soon spread around the circuit that Cleveland would be a pennant contender.

Bob felt strong and relaxed. His motion was free and easy, but the ball whammed in like a cannon shot. His curve, once a small, darting thing, now broke sharply down and out.

As usual, Feller was the hardest worker in camp. Early to bed, early to rise, careful of diet and addicted to strenuous conditioning exercises, Bob was a conversation piece among the other players.

"Don't you ever let up?" Hal Trosky asked him one day as Bob, dripping sweat, trotted in after several extra laps around the field.

"I'm a farm boy," said Bob, with a wink. "This is just play."

This powerful desire to work and improve didn't escape the restless pale blue eyes of Vitt. "I wish we had more players with his attitude," Vitt told a reporter. "Robert came over to me the other day and asked for a pitcher so he could practice bunting. Imagine any other twenty-game winner saying that!"

But while Vitt handled Feller with care during spring training, pitching him very little, he called on Bob to hurl the opener against the White Sox in Chicago. It was a bitter cold day, with an icy wind sweeping off the lake.

"Some day to pitch," Bob muttered to Hemsley as they left the dugout.

"Don't beef; it's a worse day to hit," said Rollie, noting the strong wind blowing across the plate and the dark, clouded background.

Rollie was right. With the wind behind him, Bob relied chiefly on speed and the White Sox had trouble getting wood on the ball. Inning after inning he set them down without a safety. From the fourth to the eighth, Bob retired fifteen men in a row.

The Indians scored in the fourth on Heath's single and Hemsley's blasting triple to right.

By the ninth inning, the crowd of 14,000 buzzed with excitement. The young plowboy pitcher was on the verge of the first opening day no-hitter in modern major league baseball.

Up in a box, the Feller clan sat tense and worried. Bill Feller gnawed on his lips, his face creased with anxiety. His wife sat perfectly still, almost breathless. Even young Marguerite this time sensed the drama surrounding her.

Bob got the first two men up in the ninth, but Luke Appling was proving tough. He fouled off four straight smashes until Bob finally walked him on the tenth pitch.

In the dugout, Vitt fidgeted and squirmed, slapping his knees and peering nervously into the bullpen.

Comiskey Park was silent as Taft Wright came to bat. Bob wasted no time. He glanced at Appling on first, then pitched, fast and inside. Wright swung. There was a sharp crack and the ball shot between first and second, apparently free and clear.

The crowd groaned, then cheered as Mack, off like a sprinter, sped to his left, stabbed desperately at the last moment, and knocked the ball down. Quickly he pounced on it and flung it to Trosky at first for the third out.

Everyone in the park seemed to descend on Feller, pounding and shouting congratulations. Bob managed a weak wave to his folks before he was swept into the dugout.

Later, in the solitude of the locker room after his shower and rub, Bob turned to Hemsley, dressed and waiting for the pitcher.

Bob said nothing, merely shrugging and grinning.

"What's the joke?" Rollie asked.

"The no-hitter," Bob answered. "It's hard to figure. . . . Honestly, I wasn't much today."

Rollie only grunted. Bob continued, almost to himself:

"My curve wasn't breaking right. I walked five and struck out only eight. I've been a lot faster . . ."

"You complaining?" Rollie asked sourly.

"Nope," Bob sighed. "I guess I'll take it . . . but why can't I do it on a day I'm feeling right?"

It was a buoyant start for the Indians, who followed it up with several smashing performances. The hostility toward Vitt was forgotten for a while, but slowly the old feelings were revived.

Vitt was too explosive and too hard a loser for his own

good. He was critical, too frankly so, and extremely volatile. He couldn't control his anger at errors or boner plays. The players felt he ridiculed them in public and made them the butts of his clownish jokes.

Everything was under control as the Tribe won at home and through the east. Feller had a no-hitter going against the Yankees until the seventh inning, when DiMaggio spoiled it with a drive through short. The Indians came home 1½ games behind first-place Boston and stayed with the Red Sox through June.

The first signs of trouble came in the second swing through the east. The Indians gained only an even split in eight games against the cellar teams. Vitt began pacing the dugout in furious fashion again, dropping a string of highly irritating remarks.

The situation became unbearable in New York, where the Yankees, struggling through a horrible season close to the bottom of the league, won two out of three and plastered Feller unmercifully.

Aboard the train speeding toward Boston, the Indians felt they had had enough. "Get rid of Vitt," someone said, "and we can win the pennant." But Bob was one of several who counseled caution.

Vitt was at his vituperative best the next day as the Red Sox pounded Feller. "Is that my ace?" the enraged pilot asked sarcastically.

The explosion came the next day when Boston won again on a six-run rally in the eighth which chased Al Milnar and Mel Harder. They as well as several others felt the excoriating whip of Vitt's bitter tongue.

That night, on the train heading home, the players held a general meeting. It was decided to send a delegation of twelve players, headed by Harder, to see the Indian president, Alva Bradley, and explain the situation.

The delegation met with Bradley the morning of June 13, 1940. Bradley listened, asked some questions, then told them to keep it quiet while he studied the situation.

But the newspapers emblazoned the story in banner headlines the next day. As feared, in print the team's side of the story didn't read well. All over the country, the Cleveland team became known as the Cry Babies and the Boo Hoo Boys.

They were greeted in every city with showers of ripe fruit, abusive language, and ridiculing articles. In Detroit, they were pelted with eggs, tomatoes, and stones at the Michigan Central station.

Strangely, the team began winning. They led the league at the All-Star break in July, placing six men on the American League team. Feller pitched two innings, struck out three, and gave up one run in the 4 to 0 loss to the Nationals.

The Tribe opened up a six-game lead, then suddenly went into a spin. Everything went wrong. Players committed foolish errors. The sluggers didn't slug and the pitchers couldn't pitch. Feller lost a game to the Yankees by muffing his catcher's return throw.

The pennant battle now was between the Indians and the Tigers. The Cleveland club finally drew cheers in their own town when they swept a three-game series with Detroit, late in August. The Yankees, making a miraculous recovery, began roaring up from the pack, lashing murderously with their big bats.

The Bombers beat the Tribe three straight in New York and the panic broke out again. Milnar got into a fight with Earle Combs, a former Yankee outfielder now coaching at first base.

The Indians battled on grimly until September, when three straight defeats by the Tigers, including a 7 to 2 walloping of Feller, consumed their lead. Detroit, led by the explosive bats of Greenberg and Gehringer, was red hot.

But the Tribe hung on. Feller won his twenty-fifth victory with a one-hitter against Philadelphia in which he walked no one. He beat Washington two days later for his twenty-sixth, but Bob was beginning to feel tired. His teammates were tired too. The strain of the pennant fight, the feud with Vitt, and the constant abuse by fans had worn them down.

The pennant slipped away in Detroit, where the Tigers won two out of three. Feller chalked up his twenty-seventh win, hitting his second homer of the season in the process.

The coup de grâce came in Cleveland, in the final series with the Tigers. Feller lost a three hitter to unknown Floyd Giebell in a wild 2 to 0 game in which time had to be called to clear the rotten fruit off the field.

The Indians won the next two games to clinch second place, but the disappointment in the dressing room was as thick as Mississippi mud after the final out of the 1940 season.

Vitt shook hands all around in the locker room, walked out of the park, and never came back again. He accused Slapnicka of quitting on him.

For Bob, it was a sad ending, even though it had been a grand season for him. He had won twenty-seven and lost eleven, fanned 261, walked 118 in 320 innings, and posted a 2.62 earned run average.

He was the leading pitcher in the majors, one of the greatest box office attractions, a young man with a future of infinite promise.

CHAPTER TWENTY-ONE

It was an unhappy and restless winter for Bob, despite his success and the respect accorded by people in all stations of life.

Mostly it was the terrifying change in his father, now suddenly a sick man plagued by devastating headaches. Bob dreaded even to conjecture the cause or the consequences of his dad's illness.

Even the news that Vitt had been replaced by Roger Peckinpaugh, a warm and total opposite of his vitriolic predecessor, failed to cheer Feller. Neither did the war raging in Europe nor the imminent prospect of his being drafted into the armed forces, stir him.

Bob's apathy and obvious depression over his dad's condition did not escape his mother. She cornered him in the kitchen one day.

"You look so pale, Bob," she said.

He answered with a wan smile, boyish guilt on his face. They had just helped his pain-wracked father to bed. Bob had come downstairs, trembling with a nameless dread.

"When does the team go south?" she asked.

"March," he replied, tightly.

"Why don't you go down earlier, maybe to Miami or Palm Beach," she said. "Get some sun on you and have a little fun."

"How can I go away now?" he said. "With Dad like this . . ."

And how could he stay to watch Dad come apart, Bob asked himself. "You need me here," he told her.

"Nonsense," his mother said briskly. "Dad will be going to the Mayo Clinic soon anyway. He wants you to get away. He told me he's worried about you."

Bob shook his head in wonderment. "That's rich," he said. "Dad worrying about me."

Bob felt guilty leaving, but he was relieved too. He could pitch to DiMaggio with the bases loaded without a qualm, but he couldn't face this.

West Palm Beach was perfect for casting off cares. Life was gay and busy. Bob swam, he played golf, he had dates. Lying on the hot sand, with almost two months for himself, Bob relaxed. Maybe there wasn't anything seriously wrong with Dad. . . . Maybe the Mayo doctors would be able to help. . . . Bob was on the phone every day, but thus far there was nothing new to report. Hope flourished in the warm Florida sun.

Visiting a friend at Rollins College one day, Bob was introduced to a tiny, extremely attractive girl with curly chestnut hair and the warmest, bluest eyes Bob ever gazed into. She was Virginia Winther, from Waukegan, Illinois, studying for her degree at Rollins.

Bob was intrigued, then entranced, then completely captivated. She knew nothing about baseball, had never heard of Bob Feller, and in fact had never seen a game.

"I'll teach you the game," he told her.

She smiled and he added hastily, "If you care to learn."
"I'd love it," she said.

Bob saw Virginia all during his vacation and a great deal
more than anyone knew, once spring training started. They
both were twenty-two, in love, and sure of themselves.

Spring training under Peckinpaugh was pleasant and de-
void of incident. The Tribe started slowly, concentrating
more on conditioning than victories. They didn't begin to
win until the annual northern trek with the Giants.

The Indians won nine of fourteen games on the trip north,
and in Cleveland excited fans boldly talked pennant. Even
Peck, throwing managerial caution to the winds, picked his
team to win.

For two months, it seemed Peck would be right. The Tribe
led the league well into June. Feller enjoyed blazing success,
chalking up win after win until he had fifteen, including four
shutouts.

Suddenly the tide turned. The Indians, Bob included, went
into a slump. The Yankees passed them on June 25. Going
into the All-Star game in Detroit, Bob had been shelled from
the mound three straight times.

The situation improved for Bob after the All-Star break,
but not for the Indians. Feller wound up the season with a
25 to 13 record, 260 strikeouts, 194 walks, and a 3.15 earned
run average, but Cleveland finished a dismal fourth, far
astern of the Yankees.

Disillusioned and derided, Slapnicka resigned as vice-
president of the Cleveland club. Critics pointed out that the
Indians hadn't fared any better without Vitt than with him.

No one seemed to care as much, however, not even the
usually rabid Cleveland fans. World chaos was too close. The

war drums beat too fast and too loud now. Bob, like so many youths around him, wanted to enlist.

"Why wait for the draft?" he pleaded. "All the fellows are going in." But his mother dissuaded him. His father was seriously ill now, clearly unable to work, and she wanted Bob close by.

Then came Pearl Harbor, December 7, 1941.

Two days later, Bob enlisted in the Navy, as a chief petty officer in Commander Gene Tunney's physical training division. Six months at the Norfolk Training Base putting boot trainees through pushups and knee bends was enough for Bob. He wanted action. There was a shooting war on somewhere and he wanted to get behind a trigger.

Bob's request for a transfer to gunnery school was granted. In sixteen weeks he learned a lot about guns, from small bore to huge cannons. Late that winter, Bob was assigned to the newly commissioned 35,000 ton battlewagon *Alabama*.

Bob was at sea shortly after Christmas when the sad news came. His father had died, and Bob was given a ten-day leave to return home for the funeral.

As he watched his father's remains being lowered into the earth, Bob knew his last link with boyhood was gone. Life was wondrous and beautiful, but bitter and harsh, too. The tears fell from a man's eyes that day, but the grief was a heart-stricken boy's who would always recall with poignant love the gentle patience of his farmer father.

Bill Feller was buried in the family cemetery at Des Moines. Virginia and Bob were married five days later in Waukegan. "Dad wanted it this way," Bob insisted.

All the newly married couple had was a three-day honeymoon, before Bob reported back to his ship.

137

The *Alabama* headed out to sea and action in February, 1943, cruising the Atlantic on convoy duty. The gallant ship ploughed the icy waters, battled heavy seas, and slid through fog and mists.

Baseball was a forgotten game, only a word, a memory aboard the *Alabama*. Although he was Bob Feller, a major league great to the gobs, Bob felt as if he never had played the game. It was far away in the past, dim and hazy.

When the *Alabama* was called to the South Pacific, Bob found himself for a while on solid ground again, actually playing baseball. Anchored in the New Hebrides, the sailors relaxed their sea legs with softball and baseball.

Too soon, the war resumed in earnest again for Bob. The *Alabama* fought in Pacific waters for two years, in actions at the Gilbert Islands, Kwajalein, Truk, Saipan, Palau, Nauru, Formosa, Leyte, and the crucial battle of the Philippine Sea. There was Tarawa, Bougainville, Guam and the Marianas, too.

Bob commanded the gun crew on a 40-millimeter quadruple mount antiaircraft gun, the core of the *Alabama's* protection against the enemy planes. The kamikaze pilots were the most terrifying hazard to American warships.

Bob vowed he never again would complain about DiMaggio or Williams or any other slugger smashing shots past the mound, after the hell he went through aboard the *Alabama* during the Jap attacks from the air.

Many a night Bob lay sweltering in his hammock, wondering if he ever would play baseball again. Poor Dad, he thought, gone to his rest before his time. All those wonderful days learning the game, now perhaps to be wasted in a watery grave at the bottom of the Pacific.

How much harm can a three-year layoff do a pitcher's arm? The best years of his baseball life, when he should have been at his peak, were racing by, thousands of miles from a ball park.

"I'll make it all up," Bob promised himself, grimly. "If and when I get back."

Just when the men felt they were at the breaking point, where they had to get home or go mad, the *Alabama* turned east and headed for the States. When Bob marched off the *Alabama* in Seattle on January 12, 1945, he never boarded her again.

With Virginia at his side, Bob shifted to the Great Lakes Naval Station, where he became manager of the crack baseball team which rostered such big leaguers as Ken Keltner, Walker Cooper, Denny Galehouse, and Johnny Gorsica.

At first, Bob did not play. He was content to manage, and there was a tacit understanding that he would not pitch. But gradually, anxious to loosen war-stiffened muscles, Bob eased back to the mound.

When the Japs surrendered on August 14, 1945, Bob immediately put in for his discharge. With forty-four months of service and eight battle stars, he had sufficient credits to get out quickly.

Happily and proudly, Bob left the Navy on August 22.

He joined the Indians immediately. There had been some startling changes in the club. Roger Peckinpaugh now was vice-president and Lou Boudreau the manager. Only a handful of the players Bob knew still were with the team—Boudreau, Heath, Harder, Al Smith, Jim Bagby, and Gene Desautels.

Boudreau announced Feller would pitch against the Ti-

139

gers in Cleveland Stadium the next night. Close to 47,000 turned out to see the Strikeout King in his first start since Pearl Harbor changed the world.

They saw a new, leaner, harder Bob Feller on the mound. A grim, determined man who had three lost years to make up. Bob beat the Tigers 4 to 2, striking out twelve and allowing only four hits. It was a tremendous beginning. The old magic still was there, and Cleveland rooters exulted.

Bob finished the season with five wins and three losses, while the Indians closed in fifth place.

That winter, December 10 to be exact, Bob's first son, Stephen, entered the world.

A family man now, a three-year chunk taken out of his baseball life by the war, Bob set purposefully to making it up.

CHAPTER TWENTY-TWO

How does a man recapture the lost years?

It was a familiar and no less touching problem because it was shared by so many thousands of young Americans whose lives and careers were dislocated by the war.

Time is irretrievable to a baseball player. An athlete has only a limited number of years of peak service in his body. To the professional, these are the most lucrative years.

Bob didn't begrudge the three big seasons he had given up to serve his country. Nor did he complain about the seventy-five or possibly more victories which never would go into the baseball records under his name.

It was strictly business with Bob Feller, husband and father, now. Baseball business. "It cost me about $250,000," he said, discussing the war with Virginia one evening. "The trick is to make it up."

"You will," she said, smiling with the confidence of the admiring and loving wife.

Feller signed for a $50,000 salary plus a bonus based on attendance. It was a staggering sum to everyone but Bob, who could be coldly mercenary in assessing his own value to the club.

Bob was twenty-seven, had been away from the game in a military atmosphere certainly not conducive to protecting baseball muscles. The sports world was intrigued by the question he posed. Could Feller come back?

Down at Clearwater, Florida, the new Cleveland spring training base, no one worked harder or longer than Feller. He ran countless laps around the field. He slaved at calisthenics drills. He shagged flies in the outfield until his glove felt like a lead weight.

The one thing he didn't do too much was pitch. Bob knew his own arm too well to throw hard during the training period. Critical onlookers regarded this skeptically. They watched him ease the ball in and departed, saying Feller had lost his speed.

The tune changed when the season started and Feller opened in Chicago with a 1 to 0 triumph. "He went away a boy and came home a man," one locker-room wit remarked in view of Feller's workmanlike job. Bob had issued only one walk, in the ninth inning. It was a tremendously encouraging performance.

Unfortunately, he couldn't follow it up. Bob took two beatings and the carpers and doom-chasers were on him again. The insistent stories that Feller's fast ball was gone began to irk the big ex-farmboy. Condemning his arm was like slurring his character. Bob's pride was hurt.

It didn't help when only 38,000 fans came out to see the Yankee sluggers face Bob in the huge stadium in New York. It was a comparatively small attendance for a Feller game. "I'll show 'em," he vowed. He did.

One after another the mighty Yankee sluggers went down. DiMaggio, Keller, Henrich, Dickey, Gordon, Rizzuto, Stirnweiss, Etten. For nine innings Bob hurtled his fast ball past the Bombers, baffled them with crackling curves, and confounded them with sliders.

They didn't get a hit off him. Cleveland won the game 1 to 0 in the ninth when Frankie Hayes, Feller's catcher, slammed one of Floyd Bevens's offerings into the seats for a home run.

It was the second no-hitter of Feller's career and couldn't have come at a more dramatic time. The nation's baseball writers fell over their typewriters, climbing back on the Feller bandwagon.

While he seemed calm enough, Bob exulted inwardly. In the clubhouse later, answering interviewers, Bob was gracious. He didn't gloat, but he did let the reporters know he relied mainly on his fast ball. It was a sweet victory. Someone reminded Feller about the derogatory rumors that he was slowing up. Bob frowned. "Look," he said with some heat, "when the time comes I don't have it, I'll be the first to know about it."

In the Yankee quarters, DiMaggio summed it up perfectly. "Feller was simply great," jolting Joe said, "as great as I ever saw him. He deserved his no-hitter."

Analysis of the game showed how well Feller pitched. He struck out eleven batters, issued five walks, and allowed only two balls to be hit to the outfield.

If anything, the no-hitter made Feller a greater gate magnet than previously. Still, as the Indians faltered in the race, attendance dropped off in Cleveland. Working on a gate-bonus clause, Feller was relieved when the colorful and dynamic Bill Veeck bought the club for a syndicate. Veeck was a genius at stimulating customer interest.

Perhaps because he had missed out on so much during the war, Bob had become extremely money conscious. He had a string of business ventures going, cashing in on numerous endorsements and radio interviews. In July, after the All-Star game, Bob announced a seventeen-game barnstorming tour in which an all-star group of major leaguers would play the nation's top Negro ballplayers, including Satchel Paige, Jackie Robinson, and Josh Gibson.

"You have to make it while you can," Bob explained.

His business-like attitude extended to the field. Watching Boudreau being put through the paces by a photographer from a national magazine, one day, Bob nudged Lou and asked, "What are they paying you for this story?"

Boudreau stared at the pitcher. "Nothing," he answered.

"They couldn't get me to do it for nothing," Feller said.

Boudreau and the photographer gaped as Bob ambled away.

It wasn't the sort of thing to endear him to outsiders or even to his teammates. Bob was too busy negotiating contracts, cutting records, signing endorsements and what-not to chum around with the other players. The money was rolling in, but Bob wasn't having any fun or making friends.

Even the club officials felt the sting of his shrewd business mind. When Feller came in to talk contract, he was better armed for haggling than they were.

"This guy came in knowing to the penny how much he drew at the gate," Veeck once said admiringly. "He keeps check on day-to-day receipts. What a businessman!"

Obviously, Feller knew what he was worth. The next time the Yankees came into Cleveland, 74,529 spectators paid to see Feller pitch. It was this sort of box office appeal that wound up earning Bob $72,000 that season.

With the Indians faltering, the season was reduced for Feller to a quest for personal success. Bob wanted to win the most games in the league, break the strikeout record, and top the earned run averages.

Specifically, Bob wanted to surpass Rube Waddell's old record of 343 strikeouts in the 1904 season. He pursued this goal with a cold intensity that shocked the people close to him.

Late in September, when he was drawing close to the mark, Bob even complained that rival batters weren't hitting normally.

"They're just punching at my pitches," he insisted, implying it was a deliberate attempt to foil him.

Nevertheless Bob made it, winding up the campaign with 348 strikeouts. He had won twenty-six games and lost fifteen, posted a brilliant earned run average of 2.18, and walked 153. He worked forty-eight games and pitched 371 innings, far more than anyone else.

Firm as he was in his business negotiations, Bob also was scrupulously fair and honest. "Feller is the easiest ballplayer I ever dealt with," Veeck testified. So did the executives of the varied organizations with whom Bob had contact.

Bob hadn't changed much physically. At twenty-eight, he still had a trace of the "fat-faced country boy" look, the same strolly swagger, the pouty lips and deep-dimpled chin. He managed his body as efficiently as his business enterprises. He slept nine hours a night, trained conscientiously, and worked by schedule.

The Fellers lived in a luxurious apartment in Cleveland's

plushest suburban area during the season. Bob drove a Cadillac, his wife a Buick convertible. Bob piloted his own four-passenger plane and owned a cabin cruiser. He had come a long way since his farm days in Iowa.

Although he drove a hard bargain, Bob was generous in his quiet way. For several years, unknown to even his closest friends, he had provided money for four scholarships to a small college near his old home in Iowa. After the war, he had run a free baseball school for veterans.

This was success in the best American tradition. But underneath, Bob was proudest and happiest about his baseball performances. It was still fun to be paid for playing baseball.

"Don't tell anyone, Mom," he confided one day, "but if necessary, I'd play for nothing."

His mother's brows rose in mock skepticism, then she burst out laughing. "I think you would," she agreed. "You really would."

They were silent for a while, then she spoke again.

"It's funny, isn't it," she said softly, almost to herself, "how your father was right all the time and the rest of us were wrong."

Bob nodded soberly, the sadness always there when he thought of his dad.

"He was so proud and so happy," she sighed. "At least he had that. . . ." She wiped away a tear.

"I often wonder if you'd be playing now if it weren't for him," she continued. "I guess you would. It's in the blood." She smiled and put her hand on Bob's. He looked like such a little boy at this moment.

146

CHAPTER TWENTY-THREE

It was early in the spring of 1947, and some of the boys were sitting around in Bob's hotel room.

"How's the book selling?" someone asked. Bob had just written a book, *Strikeout Story*.

"I'd better start striking someone out," Bob said, "or there won't be any sales." Bob, in his usual fashion, hadn't been too impressive during the spring exhibition games.

"Don't worry, Bob," said Felix Mackiewicz, a big rookie outfielder not long out of Purdue University, "at least you've been scattering those hits nicely. Some inside the park and some outside!"

The gang laughed along with Bob. "You'll never catch me bearing down in the spring," he retorted. "Not any more. It's the fastest way to ruin your arm."

Feller didn't get off to a good start that season. Poor spring weather and a batch of twilight double-headers slowed his progress. But gradually, as the days warmed, Bob felt loose and the strength was back in his arm again.

One night in Philadelphia, Bob was at his peak. The ball seemed to flow off his fingers and whoosh over the plate. Feeling as he did, Bob just poured in the fast ball.

The batters were slow and helpless against his pitches, which seemed to explode into the mitt. Nine of the first ten hitters struck out and the odd man bunted. Barney McCosky was up. Two strikes blazed letter-high across the plate.

Now the catcher called for a curve. Throwing mostly fast balls, Bob's left foot had worked a little ridge into the mound. For his curve, Feller usually stepped three or four inches farther to the left.

Hurling the bender to McCosky, Bob stepped down heavily into the loose dirt. The footing gave way just as he put all his weight into the throw. The fans gasped in amazement as Bob slipped violently, flipped in a complete somersault, and landed flat on his back.

Boudreau was the first to reach Feller, deathly afraid of what he would find. It had been a violent fall. "Are you all right, Bob?" he asked.

Bob rose shakily, kneading his right shoulder.

"I don't know," he said. "The shoulder hurts and my knee—whew, I can't walk on it."

Boudreau nodded grimly. "Better get inside and take a look," he said.

Oddly, the final pitch had snapped across the plate for Feller's tenth strikeout.

Bob never felt the same after that pitch. When he started pitching again, the torn ligaments in his knee healed and the knotted shoulder muscle apparently loosened, the speed was gone from his fast ball.

"Hold back on the fast ball," Boudreau advised. "Show it once in a while, but work on the curve and control. That way the big hitters won't know you've lost your fast ball. Use your head and you'll outsmart them for a couple of years."

It was tough going for Bob after that. He pitched in streaks. Two or three games would go well, then the next three would be disastrous.

He didn't win a game for close to four weeks after beating the Yankees in mid-May. The newspapers were on him and on the club for overworking Feller. He needed a vacation, they wrote.

"Nonsense," Bob said. "I'm not tired and I'm getting plenty of rest." That was for the benefit of critics who suggested Bob was spending too much time on outside business activities.

"My shoulder is tight," he explained, "and maybe I've been holding back unconsciously." Despite his explanation, Bob was worried, too. He stopped throwing between mound appearances and he halted his usual calisthenics regimen.

Bob felt like a heel, begging off the All-Star game in Chicago. Characteristically, he made no excuses to the press.

"My back hurts and I can't pitch," he told the chroniclers. "I won't be any use to the team." Neither the press nor the fans took it too kindly.

Hot weather and a consequent easing of the muscle condition found Bob back on the winning trail again—and the object of considerable wrath. The press and the public, flooded with stories of his financial manipulations, put one and one together to get three. Now they were sure tycoon Feller had been too busy to appear.

After late July, Feller lost only two games. By then, he was back on a regular four-day rotation schedule. Around the league, the players regarded him with awe as well as respect, but the fans were less bemused. They booed heartily when Bob pitched poorly.

Another son, Martin, was born to the Fellers during the season. They lived in a new home in the Cleveland suburbs, a home estimated as worth $125,000 and replete with every gadget known to home science.

The 1947 season closed with Bob a twenty-game winner against eleven losses and a sharp drop in strikeout production. Bob fanned only 196, still best in the league but well below his previous full-seasoned figures. On the other hand, he issued less passes, 127, and his 2.68 earned run average was a powerful argument in salary discussions.

Ever since his tumble on the mound in Philadelphia, Bob realized he was not the same pitcher. Going into the 1948 campaign, he set new goals for himself.

"All I want to do is win games," he told Boudreau on the ride north from spring training. "I've got about fourteen records now. Even if I could break more, it's too tough and not worth it. I want to help the team more than ever this year. I just feel that we might take the pennant, if I can win again."

Boudreau couldn't agree more heartily. "Just win 'em, Bob," the young manager said. "You do your share and I think we could take it this year."

"Yeah," Boudreau insisted. "We've got enough power, fielding, and maybe pitching. You'd like to get into the Series, wouldn't you?"

What a question, Feller thought. God, how he longed to win a Series game. It was the one ambition he hadn't realized.

"Lou, I'd break my arm off at the shoulder to win a World Series game."

Boudreau didn't doubt Feller's sincerity.

Although the Indians got off to a good start, Bob didn't. He wasn't fogging the ball in Old Bullet Bob style. The batters teed off on his high hard one.

"I'm a control pitcher now," he growled to Muddy Ruel, the old catcher, now the Tribe's battery coach. "When I've got control," he added bitterly.

Bob worked at it relentlessly, getting to where he could pinpoint the pitch. He spent hours perfecting a slider, which is only a wrinkle compared to a curve but apparently effective enough to throw hitters off their batting stride.

By mid-June, Bob had won only five games and lost seven. Worse still, he had been knocked out of the box several times. Strangely, the Indians managed to stay on top of the league race despite weak pitching.

Boudreau insisted he would ride along with Feller. "If Bob can't win," Lou said, "we're finished in the pennant race. We'll sink or swim with Feller. He's our ace and I'm going to use him every fourth day."

In the clubhouse, Boudreau cornered Feller.

"Look, Bob," he said, "you're pressing. You've gotta relax. From now on, don't even hold a ball until the day you pitch."

"I can't figure it, Lou," Bob said in a puzzled tone. "I seem to have my stuff, but I can't get those guys out."

Ruel couldn't put his finger on the trouble, either. "There's nothing wrong with his arm," Muddy told Boudreau later. "He's loose and he's strong. Personally, I think he'll snap out of it."

Ruel was right, but it took almost another two months to bear him out.

Meanwhile, harried by criticism of his business dealings, Bob announced he would forego all outside activities to concentrate on baseball. "I'm not even thinking about barnstorming after the season," he conceded.

"Besides," he noted realistically, "who'd want to see me with the kind of record I've had so far?"

Constant work, rigorous conditions and application finally told. Slowly Bob worked himself back into the win columns again. Life wasn't so bad after all, he reasoned.

The fun didn't last long for Bob. He and Bob Lemon, his mound teammate, were selected for the All-Star game in St. Louis.

Boudreau and Veeck, concerned more with their own pitching staff in the torrid American League race, couldn't see both hurlers going off to St. Louis.

"Suppose they both work in the game?" Veeck asked. "Who's gonna pitch for us?"

"Bob could use a four-day rest," Boudreau suggested. "How about saying you've hurt your arm, or something like that?"

"I don't think it would be right," Feller cautioned. "The fans got on me bad enough last year when my back kept me out of the game."

"Let us handle it," Veeck cut in. "I don't care what anyone thinks. Our first duty is to our own club."

"It's okay with me," Feller shrugged. "You're the boss."

The next day papers all over the country carried the story that Bob Feller had withdrawn from the All-Star game. That's all Veeck's blunt statement revealed.

The reaction was brutal. It seemed as if Feller callously was pulling out and that he didn't give a hoot about the Player's Pension Fund, which benefited from the receipts. Bob's phone rang all day and night.

Frantically, Feller tried to reach Veeck and finally got him at 1 A.M. "Get them off my back," Bob pleaded. "They think I'm ducking the game."

Veeck's belated explanation to the wire services and the Cleveland newspapers wasn't sufficient. The writers and fans figured Veeck was covering Feller. From then on, the boos grew louder.

Soon after the All-Star incident, Virginia Feller was in the stands for a night game at the Yankee Stadium when it sounded as though all 65,000 fans were hooting Bob. The insults were searing and she felt like getting up and swinging her handbag at every spectator deriding her husband.

Bob's expression was impassive, but his face was pale and his lips tight. This is unholy treatment, he thought grimly. But he took it.

It wasn't the All-Star incident alone. "Feller's had it too good," one analyst noted. "He's made money hand over fist. Everything he touches turns to gold. Plain folks, players and fans alike, resent it. They're jealous."

Bob Feller had only one answer. He pitched. He pitched and he won. Just when the Indians seemed to falter in August, Feller turned blazing hot. He reeled off seven straight victories and saved two more games in relief.

The fans, as usual, shifted in his favor. As the pressure eased, Bob relaxed. The harsh look left his face and he could smile again. Even Virginia admitted then that life would have been awfully hard to take if the tide hadn't turned.

"You were a meanie," she twitted her big husband.

"Sorry, honey," he said, hugging his pert wife. "I'll make it up to you."

153

"I don't ever want to hear them boo you like that again," she said, shuddering at the memory.

Bob said nothing as he held her tightly. He knew the base-ball public too well to make promises for it.

CHAPTER TWENTY-FOUR

The city of Boston was gray and windy the morning of October 6, 1948.

Gazing at the overcast skies through the window of his hotel high above the city, Bob wondered if the breeze would be blowing behind or into him at the ball park.

He couldn't sleep. It was too important a day, the one for which it seemed he had waited all his life. The Indians were in the World Series, playing the Boston Braves for the championship and the big pot of gold.

Last night, in this very room, Boudreau had told Bob he would pitch the Series opener against the Braves.

"I appreciate that, Lou," Feller had said, touched. After all, he had won only nineteen games for the season against twenty each by Bob Lemon and Gene Bearden, the young left-hander. "I'll give it everything," he promised.

"I know that, Bob," Boudreau nodded. The pilot wanted Feller as much for his experience and known courage under fire as for the power in his arm.

Bob had no appetite that morning, but forced himself to eat breakfast. Outwardly he appeared calm, but underneath the surface, the veteran pitcher tingled with excitement.

"Look at me," he smiled, standing in front of the hotel room mirror. "Just a big phony scaredy-cat."

In the Cleveland locker room no one said too much. Everyone was nervous. Feller was knotting his shoe laces when Joe Gordon, the ex-Yankee who had joined the Tribe, walked over.

"Let's be real rapid today, Robert," he commanded.

Bob looked up with a grin, grateful for Gordon's attempt to ease the tension.

"Feed 'em aspirins, boy," said Larry Doby, the strapping outfield slugger.

"Okay, boys," Boudreau shouted, "out on the field. And let's win it!"

Nervous and noisy, the players trooped out to the field.

Bob warmed up slowly, unmindful of the 40,000 fans in crowded Braves Field, of Happy Chandler, the Baseball Commissioner, or the political dignitaries staring at him. Bob limbered up with the concentration of a man with but one purpose—to win!

He was jittery only for a moment as the game started, but felt loose and free after his first pitch. The ball went just where Bob wanted. The curve was behaving beautifully and his fast one buzzed like a mad hornet.

The Braves couldn't touch him. The first nine men went down in order and for five innings Bob had a no-hitter. Johnny Sain, a thirty-year-old right-hander, was pitching as effectively for Boston.

Marv Rickert, a replacement outfielder hastily recalled when Jeff Heath broke his leg, singled to break the Feller spell in the sixth, for the first hit off Bob.

It stayed that way until the eighth, when Bob walked

Bill Salkeld, the first man to face him. Boston manager Billy Southworth sent Phil Masi in to run for Salkeld, and Mike McCormick sacrificed.

With Ed Stanky up, Boudreau ordered an intentional walk to set up a possible double play. But Sain popped one into the air for an easy outfield fly, bringing Tommy Holmes to the plate.

Holmes was a dangerous hitter, keen-eyed and quick. Bob breezed the first one past him for a strike, then wasted two with low curves. Holmes caught the next pitch on the end of his bat and the ball sliced down the third base line.

Keltner flung himself at the ball, but couldn't make it and Masi raced in with the only run of the game.

The Indians got four hits off Sain and had men as far as second base five times, but couldn't push the marker across.

It was heartbreaking for Bob, who had hurled and lost a two-hitter. Nine other men had pitched two-hitters in World Series history, but only one, Mort Cooper of the Cardinals, had lost.

The Indians were glum in the clubhouse, not only for the defeat but for Feller's sake. "Sorry," Gordon said, gripping Bob's shoulder expressively.

"You'll get another chance," Boudreau promised, and Lou was right. It happened in Cleveland, four days later, with the Indians leading 3 to 1 in the Series.

"Let's mop 'em up today," Lou enthused. "This one is for you, Bobby," he said.

It wasn't to be so, alas. There were 86,288 fans crammed into vast Municipal Stadium, on another gray and dismal afternoon, to see the Indians sew it up.

The Braves sailed into Feller the very first inning. Holmes

opened with a single, Alvin Dark followed suit, and Bob Elliott smashed one over the right field screen for a homer, driving in three runs.

Nelson Potter, a thirty-six-year-old American League cast-off, wasn't much better for the Braves. Dale Mitchell plastered him for a home run on the second pitch and the Indians clobbered him for four more runs in the fourth inning.

Meanwhile, Elliott had smashed another home run in the third, with no one on base. So the Tribe led 5 to 4 when Potter gave way to Warren Spahn.

The lead vanished when Salkeld hammered Feller's first pitch in the sixth for a homer. Bob sank deeper in the seventh. Holmes singled, advanced to second on a sacrifice, and scored on Torgesen's single. That was all for Feller.

Ed Kliemann, Russ Christopher, and finally ancient Satchel Paige came in, trying to stem the tide, but Boston was on a rampage. Bob was in the clubhouse when the final score came in: Boston 11, Cleveland 5.

He had failed again, possibly for the last time in a world series for him. Compounding his misery was the terrible hooting by the fans when he had been yanked. The jeers and cat-calling were deafening, as Bob walked slowly from the mound.

In the press box, even the calloused reporter winced. Bob's usually impassive face could not conceal the pain this time, and offered no excuses. "I didn't have a thing out there," he told reporters later. "Nothing. No curve. No speed. No control. Elliott hit a fast ball in the first and a curve in the third. Salkeld clouted a fast ball."

He shrugged eloquently, but the men surrounding him saw the choked expression, the sadness and defeat in his eyes, and for the first time felt an understanding sympathy for the big pitcher from Iowa.

The Indians won the Series the next day behind Lemon. There was no solace for Bob even in victory. The Indians had lost two games in the Series, both his responsibility. It was depressing.

"I know it's hard to feel bad for a guy who is so rich," one writer said, "but I do. Actually, making a lot of money is the only count against him. Feller is a nice guy, a square one."

Somehow, the lickings he had taken in the World Series and his Spartan attitude reacted favorably for him. Losing and being booed so unmercifully made him a human being in the eyes of the baseball public.

Rumors that Cleveland wanted to trade him while he still had value on the market brought more sympathy. Perhaps Veeck did toy with the idea, but nothing ever came of the trade stories.

At contract negotiations that winter, Feller for the first time in his career was not in the driver's seat. Veeck publicly proclaimed that Feller would have to take a pay cut, probably on the attendance bonus arrangement.

"I didn't have as good a season as in '47," Bob admitted, "so I guess I'm in line for a cut. But, the club drew a lot of people and made a lot of money, so there shouldn't be too much difference. I'll make out."

It didn't work out that smoothly. By late January, Feller was a holdout for the first time in his career. "We don't see eye to eye on the number of people who will watch us play," Feller said. When they finally did settle, Bob signed for terms which would earn him $67,000.

"I guess I'm just lucky," Bob told his wife that night.

159

"You'll have a great year, again, Bob," she sighed.

Although he loafed through the winter, gave up touring, and cut down his other activities tremendously, Bob did not have a good spring nor a good season. The speed was definitely gone from his fireball and, knowing that, the batters laid back and waited for Bob to put it over.

Feller's win total dipped to fifteen, his lowest since 1938, when he still was a raw rookie. He lost fourteen games and fanned only 108 batters in 211 innings. His earned run average rose to 3.75. The sports writers were writing his baseball obituary. Feller was on his way out, they figured.

So did the Cleveland management, which changed hands in November, despite repeated denials and rumors throughout the season. A Cleveland group headed by insurance executive Ellis Ryan bought the club for a sum in the vicinity of $2,500,000 and installed Hank Greenberg as general manager.

Greenberg lopped $20,000 off Feller's salary. "I'm just getting even for all the times Bob struck me out," Hank joked. Bob was still good for $45,000 a year, second only to Boudreau's $65,000 for his services as shortstop-manager.

The salary reduction cut deeper than the wallet with Bob. It was a further public indication of his dwindling value as a performer in the big leagues. He was resolved to show Greenberg, the press, and the public that he wasn't through yet.

Bob approached the 1950 season determined to make good. Always a conscientious conditioner, Bob trained even harder than ever. He ran and ran, he shagged flies in the field, pitched batting practice, and lived his normally clean life. Bob never smoked or drank.

Mel Harder, now a Cleveland pitching coach, observed

Feller with open admiration. "If determination can do it," Mel remarked one day, "Bob has to be a winner."

There was another, more subtle change in Feller which only those long familiar with him could notice. It always puzzled Bob that the public disliked him. Always honest and straightforward, he couldn't understand that the fans knew him only through the medium of his actions.

"I thought they were booing me for losing," Bob told Virginia, "but I was wrong."

His wife looked puzzled, and he continued: "It's my attitude they don't like. They see me as a cold, business-like guy who doesn't care a hoot about anything but a dollar."

"That's not true," Virginia declared hotly. "Why don't they know more about all the nice things you've done for other people. . . . Oh, it makes me so angry."

He had to laugh at her, her blue eyes blazing and tiny fists clenched in anger. "Don't worry, honey," he said. "They're gonna see a new Bob Feller out there."

Unquestionably, Bob had mellowed. While still a smart businessman, he no longer pursued money with the frantic intensity of previous years. He showed a growing sense of responsibility on the diamond, becoming in fact the Indians' Player Representative in negotiations with the major league club owners.

His pitching improved during the 1950 season; he wound up with a 16-11 record, including 119 strikeouts in 247 innings, 103 walks, and an earned run average of 3.43. More important, he became the fifty-fourth hurler in big league history to reach the 200-win mark.

Bob had finished the campaign in blazing fashion with six complete games, four of them winners. Of his eleven defeats

161

over the campaign, four were by one-run margins in well-pitched games which went the route.

"He's gone through a tough transitional stage," Coach Harder noted, "learning how to pitch with different weapons. Bob doesn't blow the ball past batters any more. The curve is his main reliance and speed only an auxiliary."

No matter what, Bob was happy. For the first time since the mound accident in 1947, his shoulder felt loose. The knotty lump present for so long finally disappeared.

"Wait, 'til next year," Bob told Harder as they packed their baseball duds. "There's still a little life left in the old boy yet."

CHAPTER TWENTY-FIVE

There was in fact a great deal of life left in this strapping old boy of thirty-two during the 1951 season.

Al Lopez, who replaced Boudreau as manager during the winter, was a worried onlooker as Feller started slowly that spring.

"I won't cut loose," Bob told the new pilot, "until it gets warm. I'm not taking any chances."

"You know best," Lopez said. Feller was one player he could be certain would be in condition when the league season opened.

Feller wasn't impressive during the early part of the spring. He was walloped hard the first time out. Patiently, he waited for the first sign of hot weather. It didn't come until the Indians hit Atlanta on the way home, but Bob's hurling was rewarding.

"The arm and the back feel wonderful," he said. "This is going to be a twenty-win season for me."

The reporters smiled. Big talk from an oldtimer, they thought, but Lopez, Harder, and the rest of the Tribe agreed with Bob. "Feller never talks through his hat," Harder pointed out. "Besides, I haven't seen him pitching so well since '48."

Feller won his first four league starts in a row before losing a game, then wrapped up six more wins. Nine of his first eleven victories were complete games and two were 8⅓ inning jobs.

How did Bob account for his rocket start?

"Runs tell the story," he modestly explained. "The boys are whacking the tar out of the ball. They've been averaging nine runs a game for me. It makes things a lot easier."

That wasn't the whole story at all, but it indicated Bob's new awareness of other people's feelings.

During that skein, Bob beat the pace-setting White Sox twice and every other club in the loop at least once. Only the Yankees and Red Sox earned decisions over him. The Yankees got only four hits off him, but Allie Reynolds pitched a no-hitter for a 1 to 0 triumph.

Earlier, in May, Bob was agonizingly scalded from his chest down to his knees in an overheated whirlpool bath in the clubhouse. Lopez blanched when he saw the terribly burned skin. Bob was in terrible pain, although swathed in unguents and wrapped in cotton.

"How soon before he can move around?" Lopez asked the doctor.

"It could be weeks," the physician answered. "He had a very serious burn. It's going to hurt merely moving around. I don't see how he can pitch until it heals."

But Bob was out at the park the next day.

"Are you crazy?" Harder argued, as Bob struggled into his uniform with obvious pain. "You'll get an infection. It'll kill you! Now go on home and rest for a couple of days, then we'll get the doc's OK."

Feller paid no attention.

"Listen," he told the veteran coach. "The team needs me now. We've got a chance for the pennant and I'm not gonna be the guy to let the club down."

He insisted on pitching the first game of a double-header the following Sunday, despite the vehement objections of Lopez and the coaches.

"The guy is just great," one of his teammates said with honest admiration, "but he's completely nuts."

Despite the pain and discomfort, Bob pitched and won one of his best games over the full nine innings against the White Sox.

"I've been around a long time," Birdie Tebbetts commented, "and never have seen anything like this for raw courage."

"I still don't know how he did it," Lopez marveled. "He wouldn't let me take him out. I asked him several times during the game."

Even Wally Bock, the trainer, felt squeamish pulling the cotton wrapping from Feller's raw flesh after the game. The other players fled from the sickening sight.

After that, no one ever could doubt where Feller stood with his Cleveland teammates.

Bob wasn't feeling any too chipper the morning of July 1, when he was scheduled to pitch the first game of a twin-bill against the Tigers at Municipal Stadium. He felt stiff in the warmup and Jim Hegan, his catcher, noticed it immediately. So did Harder.

"Take it easy today," Harder suggested. "No sense working if you don't feel right."

"Nope," Bob insisted. "I'll be all right once I warm up."

Bob managed to get the Bengals out, but he wasn't too impressive. In the third, Harder interrupted play to walk out to the mound. "Are you sure you're okay," he asked Bob. "You don't look so hot."

The Tigers picked up a run without getting a hit in the fourth to tie the score at 1 to 1. Johnny Lipon was safe on Ray Boone's bobble at short, stole second, made third on Feller's wide pickoff throw, and scooted home on George Kell's fly ball.

After Feller had set the Tigers down in the fifth, the crowd began to realize he was working on a possible no-hitter. The tension mounted as Bob safely got through the sixth, the seventh, and then the eighth, without yielding a safety.

By then the Indians were ahead 2 to 1. Big Luke Easter had banged in the first run with a grounder scoring Dale Mitchell in the first inning and then lashed a single following Sam Chapman's triple in the eighth.

The ninth was a tense inning. Everyone in the dugout knew how much Bob wanted his third no-hitter. In the stands, the fans squirmed feverishly, sweating it out with the pitcher.

Charlie Keller, the great ex-Yankee slugger, went in as a pinch hitter for Jerry Priddy and flied out to right. George Kell lifted a long fly to right. Vic Wertz, who had ruined a no-hitter for Bob Lemon with a homer in the eighth earlier in the season, strode to the plate.

Bob threw him a curve, which Vic fouled for strike one. Wertz watched the next strike zip by, then waggled his bat ferociously as Bob threw three straight balls just out of reach.

The drama centered on the mound, all eyes on Bob Feller. His third no-hitter rode on a three-and-two pitch!

In the dugout Lopez and the rest of the Indians hunched forward, rooting silently.

"Get that pitch in, get that pitch in," Harder muttered.

On the mound, Bob calmly surveyed the batter and waited for Hegan's signal. The slider!

Deliberately, Bob went into his windup. His arm went back, his left foot up . . . he hung poised for an instant as 42,000 spectators stopped breathing . . . then he threw!

The ball darted in, almost too far inside for a split second, then slid to the left across the plate. Wertz never moved his bat.

"Strike three," the umpire shouted, unheard in the roar that arose from the stands.

It was a tremendous moment for Bob, tired, wringing wet, but utterly happy. It was his third no-hitter, tying previous feats by Larry Corcoran for Chicago in the National League in 1880, 1882, and 1884 and by Cy Young for Cleveland in 1897 and for the Boston Red Sox in 1904 and 1907.

As Bob kept on winning, he ignited the entire Cleveland mound staff. Early Wynn, Bob Lemon and Mike Garcia rounded out a Big Four that wound up winning eighty games among them.

On August 13, in Cleveland, the fans threw a Bob Feller night, honoring the hurler they once booed and hooted. Then he went to the hill and beat the Tigers 2 to 1 for his nineteenth victory of the season.

"You know something?" Harder said in the locker room, later. "You didn't strike out a man tonight."

"Yeah, that's right," Hegan chimed in. "I never realized it, either."

Bob had to laugh. "Who cares?" he shrugged. "We won."

"The eleventh straight," added Harder.

"Well, I guess I'm not washed up yet," Feller said soberly.

Eight days later, Bob chalked up number twenty, blanking the Senators 6 to 0 under the lights at home. He put the Indians in first place September 3, beating the White Sox 5 to 3 for number twenty-one.

The Yankees edged out the Indians for the pennant, but Feller ended with a 22 to 8 record, the best in the majors, for a brilliant comeback. He fanned 111, walked only ninety-five and showed a 3.49 earned run average.

Sitting down to salary negotiation for the 1952 season, Feller had convincing arguments for a raise. His pitching once again led the league and Greenberg, in agreeing to a $55,000 stipend for the now-rich Iowan, said he was happy to make Feller the highest paid Cleveland player.

But there still was some of the farm boy left in Feller. He arose at eight o'clock every morning, worked up an appetite in the fully-equipped exercise room in his twelve room house in Cleveland's fashionable Gates Mills suburb, and joined Virginia and his three boys for breakfast.

Gadget-happy, Bob usually headed for his workshop in the stables, where he fiddled with whatever new accessory had come out for his car, or perhaps an addition for his motor scooter or private plane or power boat.

Bob spent a great deal of time reading, from newspapers to scientific treatises on aeronautics, psychology, and educa-

tion. He accepted a great many invitations to speak to youngsters at churches, schools, and boys' clubs.

The Cleveland baseball writers kidded him and his exer-
cising routine at their annual show, at which he was guest of
honor, feted by 600 guests as Cleveland's No. 1 player of
1951. Bob had come a long way in public esteem from those
unhappy days when it seemed no one in baseball liked Bob
Feller.

CHAPTER TWENTY-SIX

The years were beginning to run out on Feller on the diamond. The blazing speed had left his fireball even though he could pour in a fast one occasionally. At thirty-three, Bob was mellowing physically as well as emotionally.

"I'm throwing just as hard," Bob told one of the fellows that spring, "but the ball doesn't go as fast."

Nevertheless, he signed for $55,000 with Greenberg, who glowed publicly for his star pitcher. "Bob is the highest paid player on our ball club now," Hank said.

The sacroiliac condition which stemmed back to Feller's mound accident in 1947 bothered him again. There were days when it was difficult even to get out of bed, but Bob didn't complain.

He started the 1952 campaign in what must have been symbolic fashion, hurling a one-hitter, but losing 1 to 0 to Bob Cain of the St. Louis Browns.

It was a heartbreaker because Bob pitched so well, facing only twenty-eight batters all told. The Browns got their run in the first inning when Bobby Young tripled and came home on Al Rosen's fumble of Marty Marion's grounder to third.

It was the first time in American League history that two

pitchers in one game each had yielded one hit. Ironically, Cain had been the victim of Feller's no-hitter the previous year.

"Sorry," Rosen apologized to Feller in the clubhouse.

"It's okay," Feller said, solacing the unhappy infielder.

"What was that," asked a reporter, "your eleventh one-hitter?"

"Yeah," Bob answered, "but the first one I ever lost."

More disturbing than this defeat to Bob were the insistent rumors he wasn't getting along with Lopez. There didn't seem to be any way of combating the gossip. Neither his nor Lopez' denials made an impression.

It was a losing campaign for Bob, who lacked the pinpoint control of '51. Bob lost his confidence and worried, not so much for himself as for the team. The result was that the infielders, particularly anxious to protect Bob, were becoming jittery.

Finally, in September, Lopez lifted Bob from the regular rotation. The Indians were fighting the Yankees for the flag and couldn't afford to go with Feller the way he was working.

Bob closed the year with a 9 to 13 mark, his first losing one in the majors, as the Yankees went on to the pennant. Bob had fanned only eighty-one, walked eighty-three, and posted a 4.73 earned run average.

"I'm not through," he insisted. "It's just the law of averages. I pitched just as well as last year, only this time the luck went against me."

Bob recognized the fact he was getting older and couldn't expect to reach his former heights on the field. Sitting around with his wife and some of the baseball folk in Johnny Johnston's restaurant in New York one night, Bob explained how it feels to grow older in uniform.

"As you age," he said, "you lose the co-ordination that gives you the speed. You're just as strong muscularly, maybe stronger, but the timing and rhythm that go into chucking a ball past a batter are gone.

"Your consistency is gone, too. Sure, I can cut loose with a blazer every once in a while, but I can't do it consistently. I'm not even sure I'll have it when I try. So you can't take a chance serving up a fat pitch, and you go to curves, sinkers, knucklers, and what-have-you."

Someone wanted to know the best batter he'd ever faced. Bob thought it over for a few seconds.

"Hornsby, I guess," he said at last.

"Hornsby?" his wife questioned. "I didn't know you ever pitched to him."

"Getting to be quite a baseball expert, isn't she?" Bob kidded. "Yes, he was managing in '36 and '37 when I came up. I'd say he was the best right-handed hitter and Al Simmons next."

"How about DiMaggio?" Was he agreeing with Ty Cobb that DiMag didn't rate with the all-time greats?

"I didn't say that," Feller responded. "Joe was great in every respect—throwing, fielding, and hitting. At bat I'd compare him to Simmons. But not with Hornsby. Not even Ted Williams, the toughest lefty hitter I ever pitched to, rates with Hornsby."

Bob wasn't impressive during the spring of 1953, which led to widespread stories again that he and Lopez were at odds.

Never one to strain during the spring workouts, Bob was

pitching in an exhibition against the Pirates in San Bernardino, California, and not doing too well.

Lopez, seated on a bench directly in front of a reporter, shook his head at the performance. "He'll never get anyone out, throwing like that," Lopez half muttered to no one in particular. It was an idle remark, without implication. Lopez knew Feller's slow training method.

The reporter behind him, however, didn't. He blew it up to a scare story in which he had Lopez incensed by Feller's loafing. Al was aghast at the scope and circulation of the article.

"Bob," he said sincerely, "I never said anything like it. I don't feel that way about you and never have. If everyone gave out 100 per cent like you, we'd never lose a pennant."

It was obvious that Feller's days as a regular starter were about over. "I'm still figuring on a lot of good work from Bob," Lopez told reporters. "He's due for a couple of good breaks he didn't get last season."

Harder, the coach, put his finger on the situation.

"Bob isn't washed up," Mel pointed out. "He's good for ten to twelve wins a season. The physical strain of winning twenty is too much for him now. He's at the stage where a pitcher needs more rest between assignments."

Harder was right. Bob won ten and lost seven, working mostly in spots, as the Indians again trailed the Yankees in the pennant race.

"It's not as much fun when you don't play enough," Bob admitted, "but it's better than not playing at all."

"Are you ever going to get this game out of your blood?" Virginia asked him one night.

173

"Never," he answered immediately. "It's the sap that runs through my family tree."

The 1954 season was the last good one and in a way the most disappointing of Feller's career. He won thirteen and lost three as the Tribe finally snared the pennant. In mid-July, Bob hurled a 6 to o two-hitter in which Don Bollweg, who got both safeties, was the only man to reach base.

The Giants, the Indians' old springtime buddies, won in the National League to become their World Series foes.

"This is what I've been waiting for," Bob said. "It's my chance to win a world series game."

"You'll make it this time," Harder promised.

Lopez agreed. The canny pilot figured he would use Lemon, Wynn, Garcia, and then Feller in the fourth game.

But it never worked out that way. The Giants, led by Willie Mays, went berserk. They took the first three games in a row and Lopez, desperate, had to switch plans.

He hated to break the news to Feller.

"I'll tell him," Harder volunteered, but Lopez shook him off.

Al dropped into Feller's room that night. Bob knew it was bad news as soon as he spied Lopez' strained features.

"I know how much you're counting on this," the manager began, "but I can't start you tomorrow. We've gotta win to stay alive and I'm going with Lemon."

Bob swallowed and then shrugged. "I appreciate you telling me," he said, after a while. "If it's for the team . . . I wouldn't want to pitch unless you felt I could win."

Lopez left with enhanced admiration for Feller. "He's got character," Lopez told Harder later.

Bob never got his chance to work in the Series. The Giants

blasted Lemon to make it four in a row and the Series was over.

"That's it," Bob said, glumly driving back to the hotel with his wife. "I guess that's one record I'll never make."

Virginia knew what he meant and remained silent. There are no solacing words for that situation.

Lopez was on the spot all winter, explaining why he hadn't used Feller.

"I just didn't think he could stop that hot ball club," Al insisted. "Maybe he would have stopped 'em cold. But that's only second-guessing. My best pitcher was Lemon, and I had to pick him in the crisis."

Bob signed for 1955 at a salary of $30,000, admitting he would be satisfied to match his 1954 record. "I figure I can do the team some good the next two or three years," he said. "I feel wonderful now."

On May 1, Feller indicated how effective he still could be by shutting out Boston 2 to 0 with the twelfth one-hitter of his career. Only Sam White's single in the seventh inning spoiled a fourth no-hitter for the big-boned veteran.

On the same double-header bill, young Herb Score, the left-handed speedball chucker, fanned sixteen as he beat Boston 2 to 1. Watching Score, Bob was reminded of his own young days when the dynamite still was in his arm. Score was the new strikeout king, Feller the old one.

It was not a happy season for Feller. After his one-hitter against the Red Sox, Bob did not face a first division club again. His only other complete game was a four-hitter against Baltimore late in June. Lopez had lost confidence in Bob, both as a starter and reliever.

Feller was never brought in with men on bases. He would

get into action only to head off the opposition until another flinger could be warmed up or a pinch hitter inserted. It was a humbling experience for a player of Feller's experience and background.

His record was a mere 4 to 4 for 1955, his strikeout total dwindled now, to twenty-five. In 1956, it was 0 to 4 with only eight strikeouts.

In a way, Bob was something of a phenomenon. At thirty-seven, he showed no sign of the erosion of time. His body was firm, his skin clear and fresh, his hair black, his weight the same as always. Outwardly, there had been no change.

CHAPTER TWENTY-SEVEN

As Feller's value as a pitcher diminished, his worth to baseball in other directions blossomed. When Allie Reynolds of the Yankees left the game in 1955, Bob became the American League Player Representative.

Regarded as something of a financial genius by other ballplayers and highly respected for his integrity, Bob was a natural to represent the teams in negotiations with the owners. Equally important, Feller wasn't afraid to speak his mind.

Feller approached his duties as Player Representative with intelligence and zeal. The owners soon realized that Feller was thoroughly familiar with the business end of baseball. He led the battle to solidify the pension fund through radio and television rights to the All-Star game and World Series.

"It's surprising," he told some non-baseball friends, one evening, "how little most people know about our labor-management setup in big league baseball."

"Well, it's pretty hard to think of a ballplayer as a wage slave," someone pointed out. "After all, the hours are so good!"

"Are they?" asked Feller. "A player puts in a lot of hard

work and long hours. Playing ball for fun and playing ball for a living are completely different things."

Once started, Feller had a lot to say about big league baseball. Bob loved the game so dearly and had become so much a part of it that he understood its intricacies as a master engineer knows his engines.

He realized how one-sided a life baseball could be for the average performer who knew no other trade or business and didn't prepare for life after his league days were finished. He knew the thousand-and-one extra expenses a ballplayer encounters and how quickly the "easy" money is spent.

Bob had several pet theories for helping the players. He wanted to set up an educational arrangement with three top universities, one each in the East, Midwest, and West Coast, whereby special courses would be offered to pro ballplayers.

He wanted an employment and guidance office established in every city which possessed a big league team, conducted by local businessmen. "A ballplayer can offer prestige value to any business staff," Bob argued.

Everything he did pointed to one thing: that Feller thought the game belonged to the ballplayers first, then, to the owners and fans. "What is baseball without the players?" he asked.

His role as Player Representative took on increasing importance to Feller as his pitching prestige waned. "It gives me a chance to get up and say the things about the game I feel should be said," he told his friends.

"Why don't you quit?" a friend asked him. "You aren't getting any younger or any better. What's the sense of hanging on?"

"It's not that easy," Bob said ruefully. "It's been my life

so long, I don't know what I'd do or how I'd feel out of it."

"You've got enough businesses to keep you going twenty-four hours a day," he was told.

"Yes, I suppose the day is getting near," Bob sighed.

Rumors started that Bob Feller was being traded. Bob Feller would become a coach. Bob Feller was quitting.

Bob avoided answering them as much as possible. Through the winter, he spent most of his time in Hartford, Connecticut, learning the insurance business, in which he had heavy investments.

On December 28, 1956, Feller called a press conference at the offices of the Cleveland Indians.

"Gentlemen," he said to the hordes of newsmen and officials, "I'm retiring from baseball."

There was an excited hum, even though by that time everyone expected the statement.

"I intend to devote more time to my insurance business and at least fifty days a year to a youth project dealing with baseball."

Bob made his announcement quietly and humbly. The reporters, many of whom in previous years had displayed open dislike, now felt the sadness of the moment with the still young-looking thirty-eight-year-old man.

"It's funny, Bob," one remarked, "that with this announcement, you turn from an old ballplayer to a young executive."

Later, Hank Greenberg, speaking for the Cleveland club, revealed that Bob's number 19 would be retired, an honor no other Indian player ever had been accorded.

"I could have gone with a couple of other clubs," Bob said. "But anything I would have done would have been anticlimactic. I've been with the Indians twenty years, so I may as well finish with them."

Although he would have to abandon his position as Player Representative in the American League, Feller continued as president of the newly organized Major League Players Association and as a member of the Major League Pension Committee.

"How about taking a front-office job with the club," someone asked.

"After careful consideration," Feller said, "I have decided it would not be best for my family. Building up my insurance business and other interests would mean more financially."

So ended a fabulous baseball career, which started at the age of seven behind the barn on a farm in Iowa.

Robert "Rapid" Feller retired from professional baseball in 1956. In twenty-one years of major league ball, interrupted only by the three-year stint he did in the Armed Services of the United States, he had pitched in 569 games, a total of 3,828 innings, and had struck out 2,681 batters in winning 266 games for his ball club. He could sit back in his den and contemplate with just satisfaction the long years of service he had given to the Cleveland Indians, the thrill-packed years he had given to the Cleveland fans.

"He throws them harder than anyone since Walter Johnson pitched them for the Washington Senators," the old-timers used to say.

"No one pitched them harder than Bob Feller," say the younger fans; and some of those who had watched the big Walter Johnson in action weren't quick to dispute it.

Bob Feller pitched three no-hitters. He pitched twelve games in which his opponents could do no better than collect a single, solitary hit, for all their mighty efforts at the plate.

"Only two other men in the big leagues pitched three no-hit games," says Steve Feller, Bob's sixteen-year-old son. No one can deny that; it's a fact.

"And no one pitched as many as twelve one-hitters," adds his fourteen-year-old son, Marty.

"That's the record," says Bob Feller.

He smiles.

"Roger Maris broke Babe Ruth's record. They'll break mine."

"Maybe," says Steve Feller, swinging his bat.

Steve follows in his father's footsteps. His heart is set on the diamond. Marty is more interested in football. Both boys, however, are most proud of their dad, have always been proud of their dad and, today, they have more reason than ever for their pride.

When a man leaves his greatness on the diamond, there is only one place it can be picked up again: the National Baseball Hall of Fame in Cooperstown, New York. Once every year, members of the Baseball Writers' Association of America of at least ten years' standing cast their ballots and a name—sometimes two names, sometimes no name at all—is added to the list of baseball's immortals.

In 1956, the slugging Hank Greenberg and the great Joe Cronin were elected to the Cooperstown Hall of Fame. In 1957, the baseball writers added no one to that eternal roster. Nor was there another name added to baseball's Hall of Fame for the next four years.

In 1962, Robert "Rapid" Feller became eligible for election

to that great assemblage of baseball heroes immortalized in Cooperstown.

The writers met. They cast their ballots: 160. One hundred and twenty, or seventy-five per cent of the ballots cast, were necessary to name a man to the scroll of honor. Robert "Rapid" Feller earned 150 of them. His was the honor, and forever his name will be engraved among those whom the baseball world considers, respects, and glorifies as the greatest of heroes the world of baseball has given to America.

How does a man feel, when his accomplishments are so signally recognized and honored?

"This is my greatest season since 1946," said Bob Feller.

In 1946, he had pitched 371 innings, struck out 348 men, and won twenty-six games for Cleveland.

More seriously, he said, "This winds up my baseball career. Nothing that went before matches this thrill."

Ultimately, however, the thrill is baseball's. It is the thrill that comes with giving to its great the greatness due them. No man gave more of himself to baseball than Bob Feller. Baseball could do no less than to elect to its Hall of Fame that great man, that great heart of the diamond, Bob Feller.

FELLER'S RECORD

FELLER'S RECORD

Year	Games	Innings Pitched	Won	Lost	Percentage	Strike-outs	Bases on Balls	Earned Run Average
1936	14	62	5	3	.625	76	47	3.34
1937	26	149	9	7	.563	150	106	3.38
1938	38	278	17	11	.607	340	208	4.08
1939	39	297	24	9	.727	246	142	2.85
1940	43	320	27	11	.711	261	118	2.62
1941	44	343	25	13	.658	260	194	3.15
1942, 1943 and 1944 in the service.								
1945	9	72	5	3	.625	59	35	2.50
1946	48	371	26	15	.634	348	153	2.18
1947	42	299	20	11	.645	196	127	2.68
1948	44	280	19	15	.559	164	116	3.57
1949	36	211	15	14	.517	108	84	3.75
1950	35	247	16	11	.593	119	103	3.43
1951	33	250	22	8	.733	111	95	3.49
1952	30	192	9	13	.409	81	83	4.73
1953	25	176	10	7	.588	60	60	3.58
1954	19	140	13	3	.813	59	39	3.09
1955	25	83	4	4	.500	25	31	3.47
1956	19	58	0	4	.000	18	4	4.97
Totals	569	3828	266	162	.609	2681	1745	3.24

WORLD SERIES

1948	8	14⅓	0	2	.000	7	5	5.02

ALL-STAR GAMES

1939		3⅔	0	0	.000	2	1	0.00
1940		2	0	0	.000	3	2	4.50
1941		3	0	0	.000	4	0	0.00
1946		3	1	0	1.000	3	0	0.00
1950		⅔	0	0	.000	1	1	0.00
Totals		12⅔	1	0	1.000	13	4	0.73

INDEX

All-Star game, against National League, 122–23
Allen, Johnny, 61, 74, 102–3, 114, 116, 121
Appling, Luke, 128
Austin, A. L., 103–5
Averill, Earl, 61, 116, 121–22

Bagby, Jim, 139
Bartell, Dick, 99–100
Bassler, Johnny, 112
Bearden, Gene, 155
Becker, Joe, 69
Bell, Bob, 80
Bevans, Floyd, 143
Blaeholder, 74
Bock, Wally, 165
Bollweg, Don, 174
Boone, Ray, 166
Boston Braves, 1948 World Series, 156–59
Boston Red Sox, 83, 109, 116, 130, 164, 175
Bottomley, Jim, 80, 85–86
Boudreau, Lou, 124, 139, 144, 148, 150–51
Bradley, Alva, 121, 131
Bradley, Bill, 57
Bridges, Tommy, 48, 122–23

Cain, Bob, 170
Caldwell, Earl, 80
Campbell, Bruce, 61, 70
Castle, Dr. Ed, 102
Chapman, Sam, 166
Chicago White Sox, 90, 109–10, 128, 142, 164–65, 168
Christman, 119
Christopher, Russ, 158
Clift, Harland, 80
Collins, Eddie, 57
Collins, Rip, 66, 69
Combs, Earle, 132
Cooper, Mort, 157

Cooper, Walker, 139
Corcoran, Larry, 167
Cronin, Joe, 123, 181
Crosetti, Frank, 77, 84, 107
Cullenbine, 118–19

Dark, Alvin, 158
Dean, Dizzy, 48, 64, 70, 81
Dean, Paul, 48, 64
Desautels, Gene, 139
Detroit Tigers, 48, 90, 94, 106, 116, 118–19, 121, 131–32, 140, 166–67
Dickey, Bill, 77, 142
DiMaggio, Joe, 77, 84, 107–8, 110, 117, 125, 130, 142–43, 172
Doan, Ray, 111
Doby, Larry, 156
Doerr, Bobby, 122
Doyle, Bill, 57
Durocher, Leo, 64, 66–70

Easter, Big Luke, 166
Eisenstat, Harry, 118
Elliott, Bob, 158
Etten, 143

Falk, Bib, 96
Feller, Ed, 7
Feller, Marguerite, 21, 95
Feller, Martin, 150, 181
Feller, Stephen, 140, 181

Foret, Grandpa Ed, 7, 95
Foxx, Jimmy, 73, 83, 119, 125
Frisch, Frankie, 64

Galehouse, Denny, 74, 103, 139
Garcia, Mike, 167
Garibaldi, Art, 66, 68
Gehrig, Lou, 73, 77, 107–8, 110, 117
Gehringer, Charley, 48, 106, 132
Gelbert, 66, 70
George, Charles, 79
Gibson, Josh, 144
Giebell, Floyd, 132
Gomez, Lefty, 77, 84, 110, 119
Gordon, Joe, 115, 123, 142, 156–57
Gorsica, Johnny, 139
Goslin, Goose, 48
Greenberg, Hank, 48, 73, 106, 118–19, 123, 132, 160, 168, 170, 179, 181
Grove, Lefty, 20
Gumpert, Randy, 86

Hack, Stan, 123
Hale, Sammy, 61, 107
Harder, Mel, 61, 74, 101, 103, 116, 119, 121, 124, 130–31, 139, 160, 162–66, 173
Hayes, Frank, 143
Heath, Jeff, 121, 128, 139, 156
Hegan, Jim, 165

Hemsley, Rollie, 115, 121–22, 128–29
Henrich, Tommy, 142
Herring, Clyde, 95
Hoag, Myril, 109
Holmes, Tommy, 157–58
Hornsby, Rogers, 20, 79, 81, 102, 172
Hubbell, Carl, 99–101
Huggins, Miller, 22
Hunter, Fred, 57

Johnson, Walter, 49, 180
Jungman, John, 94–95

Kell, George, 166
Keller, Charlie, 142, 166
Keltner, Ken, 139, 157
Keyse, Lee, 91
Kliemann, Ed, 158
Knickerbocker, Billy, 101
Kress, Red, 75

Laabs, Chet, 119
Landis, Judge Kenesaw Mountain, 89, 91–93, 96
Lary, Lyn, 80, 85
Lazzeri, Tony, 77, 84
Leiber, Hank, 100
Lemon, Bob, 152, 155, 159, 166–67
Lipon, Johnny, 166
Lopez, Al, 163–65, 173, 175

Mack, Connie, 86
Mack, Ray, 124, 129
Mackiewicz, Felix, 147
Marion, Marty, 170
Maris, Roger, 181
Martin, Pepper, 48, 64, 68–69
Martin, Stu, 66, 68
Masi, Phil, 157
Mays, Willie, 174
McCarthy, Joe, 122–23
McCormick, Mike, 157
McCosky, Barney, 148
McGraw, John, 22
Medwick, Joe, 64, 66
Milnar, Al, 130, 132
Mitchell, Dale, 158, 166
Mize, Johnny, 123
Monohan, Pat, 57
Moore, Terry, 64, 66, 68
Moss, Charlie, 87
Munns, 66, 68, 70
Murphy, Johnny, 77

New York Giants, 99, 113, 136, 174
    1954 World Series, 174–75
New York Yankees, 77–78, 86, 99, 106–10, 115–17, 122, 124, 130–32, 136, 142–43, 164, 168, 171
Newark Bears, 111
Newsom, Bobo, 119

Ogrodowski, Bruce, 66–67, 69
O'Neill, Steve, 65, 111
O'Rourke, Steve, 57
Ott, Mel, 99, 123–24

Paige, Satchel, 144, 158
Pearson, Monte, 79
Peckinpaugh, Roger, 134, 136, 139
Philadelphia Athletics, 74, 86–87, 108, 132, 147–48
Pittsburgh Pirates, 173
Potter, Nelson, 158
Priddy, Jerry, 166
Pucinelli, George, 87
Pytlak, Frank, 79, 101, 107, 118, 121

Reynolds, Allie, 164, 176
Rickert, Marv, 156
Rickey, Frank, 57
Rizzuto, Phil, 142
Robinson, Jackie, 144
Rolfe, Red, 77, 107
Rosen, Al, 170
Rowe, "Schoolboy," 48
Ruel, Muddy, 151
Ruffing, Red, 77, 107, 119
Ruth, Babe, 20, 73
Ryan, Ellis, 160

Sain, Johnny, 156–57
St. Louis Browns, 79–81, 85, 101, 109, 114, 170
St. Louis Cardinals, 48, Exhibition game with Cleveland Indians, 66–70
Salkeld, Bill, 157–58
Saltzgaver, Jackie, 84
Schang, Wally, 72–74, 112
Score, Herb, 175
Simmons, Al, 172
Slapnicka, Cyril, 50–51, 136
Smith, Al, 139
Sotters, Julie, 80
Southworth, Billy, 157
Spahn, Warren, 158
Speaker, Tris, 62
Stanky, Ed, 157
Stirnweiss, 142–43
Sullivan, Billy, 75, 114

Tebbetts, Birdie, 118–19, 165
Terry, Bill, 99
Torgesen, 158
Trosky, Hal, 60–61, 70, 80, 87, 127
Tunney, Gene, 137

Uhle, George, 66

Vaughan, Arky, 123
Veeck, 59, 143–45
Vitt, Oscar, 111–13, 116–17, 121, 124, 127–30, 132

Waddell, Rube, 81, 145

Washington Senators, 74–75, 85, 108–9, 132, 168

Weatheraly, Roy, 78, 82, 87

Weisman, Max (Lefty), 61–62, 70, 73

Wertz, Vic, 166

West, Sam, 80, 86

Wetzel, Buzz, 57

White, Sam, 175

Whitehill, Earl, 96, 103

Williams, Ted, 172

Winther, Virginia, 135–37

Wright, Taft, 129

Wynn, Early, 167

Young, Bobby, 170

Young, Cy, 167